W9-BVL-985

Hyena and the Moon

World Folklore Series

Heather McNeil, Series Editor

No. 1   *Folk Stories of the Hmong: Peoples of Laos, Thailand, and Vietnam.* By Norma J. Livo and Dia Cha.

No. 2   *Images of a People: Tlingit Myths and Legends.* By Mary Helen Pelton and Jacqueline DiGennaro.

No. 3   *Hyena and the Moon: Stories to Tell from Kenya.* By Heather McNeil.

No. 4   *The Corn Woman: Stories and Legends of the Hispanic Southwest.* Retold by Angel Vigil.

No. 5.   *Thai Tales: Folktales of Thailand.* Retold by Supaporn Vathanaprida. Edited by Margaret Read MacDonald.

Hyena and the Moon
Stories to Tell from Kenya

HEATHER McNEIL

Libraries Unlimited, Inc.
Englewood, Colorado

1994

LIBRARIES UNLIMITED, INC.
P.O. Box 6633
Englewood, CO 80155-6633
1-800-237-6124

Photography: Heather McNeil
Interior book design and type selection: Judy Gay Matthews
Original art work: Joan Garner

Project Editor: Stephen Haenel
Copy Editor: Deborah Korte
Proofreader: Richard Haight
Typesetter: Kay Minnis

Library of Congress Cataloging-in-Publication Data

McNeil, Heather.
    Hyena and the moon : stories to tell from Kenya / Heather McNeil.
    xv, 171 p. 19x26 cm.
    Includes bibliographical references and index.
    ISBN 1-56308-169-5
    1. Tales--Kenya. I. Title.
GR356.4.M36   1994
398.2'096762--dc20   93-44320
                                                                CIP

This book is dedicated to
my parents,
who have always believed in me
and in dreams coming true.

Kanga—a cloth worn by women.

Contents

Preface ix

Acknowledgments xiii

Travels Through Kenya (map) xv

Stories from the Kikuyu 1

    Who Are the Kikuyu? 3
    From My Journal 10
    The Boy Who Went to Heaven 14
    Original Translation 18
    Notes and Tips on the Telling 19
    Rabbit and Lion 21
    Original Translation 25
    Tips on the Telling 26

Stories from the Turkana 27

    Who Are the Turkana? 29
    From My Journal 31
    Not So! 33
    Original Translation (Turkana) 38
    Original Translation (Samburu) 39
    Notes and Tips on the Telling 40

Stories from the Akamba 41

    Who Are the Akamba? 43
    From My Journal 46
    Peace and Quiet 49
    Original Translation 53
    Tips on the Telling 54

Stories from the Kipsigis 55

    Who Are the Kipsigis? 57
    From My Journal 60
    Monkey's Feast 63
    Original Translation 67
    Notes and Tips on the Telling 68

Stories from the Taita 71

    Who Are the Taita? 73
    From My Journal 77
    Rabbit's Drum 80
    Original Translation 83
    Notes and Tips on the Telling 84
    Water, Water Will Be Mine 86
    Original Translation 95
    Tips on the Telling 96

Stories from the Luhya 97

    Who Are the Luhya? 99
    From My Journal 100
    Ripe Fruit 103
    Original Translation (Luhya) 105
    Original Translation (Kikuyu) 106
    Notes and Tips on the Telling 107

Stories from the Samburu 109

    Who Are the Samburu? 111
    From My Journal 116
    Good Luck, Bad Luck 126
    Original Translation 131
    Notes and Tips on the Telling 133
    Hyena and the Moon 134
    Original Translation 138
    Tips on the Telling 138

Last Days 141

    From My Journal 143

Contradictions and Conclusions 145

Glossary 159

Bibliography 163

    Books 163
    Pamphlets 166

Index 167

About the Author 171

Preface

"Sikilizeni hadithi yangu! Listen to my story!"

When I was ten years old, I read Joy Adamson's trilogy about Elsa the lioness. Ever since, I have believed I belong in Kenya. African stories sing to me, especially those of the savannah and the animals who survive in the wind-tossed red-oat grass.

So, after twenty-five years of dreaming, I traveled to Kenya. I went to see the lean and hungry cheetah patiently stalk an impala, and the lean and handsome Samburu warriors leap and dance. I listened to the lion hunt in the darkness, his call more of a cough than a roar, and to the dove sing in the morning with a cry that seems to echo the tribal name "ki-KU-yu." I stood among hundreds of flamingoes at dawn and looked into a leopard's eyes at sunset. I picnicked among thousands of wildebeest as they made their annual migration to the Serengeti, and I ate mangoes and sugarcane in the markets. I walked the forests of Mt. Kenya's green mansions, the rocky desert of Samburu, and the crowded, noisy, lively streets of Mombasa.

Above all, I listened to the stories. In a cornfield, under a cashew tree, inside a dung-and-mud hut, surrounded by children, goats, chickens, mothers, fathers, grandparents, great-grandparents, the old and the young, I listened to their stories. The Kenyans were generous with them, often surprised at my interest but willing to share as long as I was willing to listen. Frequently I heard, "Oh, once I knew so many stories. But now, the stories are gone."

There are more than forty different ethnic groups in Kenya, which means more than forty different languages are spoken in a country about the same size as California. Swahili is the national language, and many people speak excellent English, as well as many other European languages. But often the elderly speak only their tribal language, and I knew my negotiations for permission to hear stories would usually be with the *mzee*, male elder. So I needed a translator, and, luckily, I found Kagathi.

But Peter Kagathi Gitema was more than a translator. He is Kikuyu, a safari guide, and a wilderness survival expert. He is also a diplomat in the finest sense, sensitive to the different cultural histories, as well as any possible discomfort the people might experience in dealing with a white, single woman. He is a humorist, singer, and storyteller, and often called upon those talents to relax the listeners and acquaint them with what *mama mzungu*, white woman, wanted to hear. He loves his country and is proud to share his vast knowledge of Kenyan birds, animals, and plants. He was my companion and friend; we often left a storytelling session so excited about what we had heard that we would both shout, "*Mzuri sana!* Very well done!"

Kagathi was responsible for making contact with a potential storyteller. Wherever it seemed appropriate, he would simply ask whether anyone could tell stories to this woman from America. In the market, the bar, the petrol station, while buying a newspaper or a bundle of *miraa* leaves to chew, he would ask for stories. If someone knew a storyteller, we would travel to him or her, usually taking along the original contact person as our introduction. Kagathi would negotiate permission for me to record the stories and to take pictures after the telling [all photographs are identified with a small superscript number: [1]]. I always paid each storyteller, with an extra amount for the *mzee* and for the translator, if the stories were told in a language Kagathi did not understand.

On my first story safari I was accompanied by a journalist who hoped to find articles to write. However, she was not comfortable in Kenya and returned early; I continued alone. The next year I traveled with Susan Grant Raymond, an artist who hoped to find motivation for sculpting the people of the country. Kenya touched her as it has me. I will never forget how she trembled when she first saw the elephants appearing suddenly and silently in the dusk to visit the waterhole at The Ark. She was a good companion.

This book includes only a few of the more than 100 stories I heard. Some of the stories seemed too confused or violent. Some mean nothing outside of the culture to which they belong. Some were merely descriptions of hunting expeditions or cattle raids. As I transcribed the stories from tape to paper, I found many unexpected problems. For instance, I never realized how much of a story is perceived visually. With the teller no longer there in front of me, parts of a story made no sense. I was also unaware of competing sounds. A child cries, a rooster crows, Kagathi jingles his keys, and words, phrases, or sentences are lost. Sometimes, too, there are obvious errors in the translation.

The result is that much of the retelling is my own creation, a combination of error, knowledge, and imagination. I had to make the stories mine but still remain true to the storyteller's culture and tradition. I have included the word-for-word translations for those interested in seeing how the story came alive for me. If I heard the story more than once, from different ethnic groups, I have included all original translations so that aspiring storytellers can see how I created my own version from a weaving of all versions. There is no significance as to which ethnic group I chose for the placement of the story within this book; I simply wanted to represent each of the groups from whom I collected stories. Also provided are excerpts from my journal, explaining where and how I heard the stories, recommendations on how to tell them, and a glossary of pronunciation for Swahili words used in my retellings.

In addition, I have included information about the history of each ethnic group, with an emphasis on the traditions of long ago, because that is when the stories originated. Some of the cultures are easily researched, for much has been written; information on others is not as readily available, so my comments are brief. Also, lifestyles of modern Kenya vary greatly, and rather than assume that a tradition is or is not still in practice by a particular ethnic group, I have chosen to use past tense when writing about customs, unless my source

x
Preface

of information is recent enough to assure me that the majority of the ethnic group still follows the customs of long ago.

The stories that sang to me, those stories that said, "Tell me! Keep me alive!"—those are the stories I have rewritten, told, rewritten again, told some more, and, when the story was mine, passed them on in this book so that Kenya can sing to you.

Hadithi yangu imekwisha. My story is finished.

Acknowledgments

I would like to thank the following people for their help in making this book come true:

My father, Colonel Robert McNeil (Ret.), for believing I could use a camera and teaching me how to do so;

My mother, Bonnie McNeil, for proofreading and advising and encouraging;

My Swahili instructor, Brian Hester, for graciously correcting my errors;

The interlibrary loan staff at the Edwin A. Bemis Public Library, for finding the obscure books I needed;

Susan Grant Raymond, my traveling companion, who provided me with friendship during our storytelling safari, as well as photographs of me that prove I was there;

Peter Kagathi Gitema, my guide, storyteller, and friend, for understanding the importance of the stories.

Travels Through Kenya

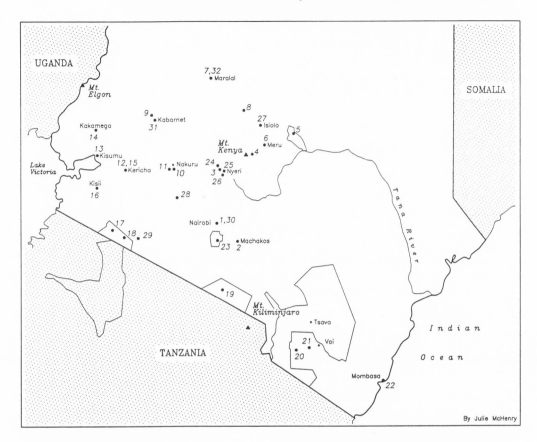

By Julie McHenry

1. Norfolk Hotel, Nairobi
2. Machakos (Akamba)
3. Treetops Lodge, Aberdare National Park
4. Naro Moru River Lodge, Mt. Kenya National Park (Kikuyu and Akamba)
5. Naro Maruko Lodge, Meru National Park
6. Meru (Meru)
7. Maralal (Samburu)
8. Samburu Game Lodge, Samburu National Reserve (Samburu; Njemps; Pokot; Turkana)
9. Lake Baringo Lodge, Lake Baringo
10. Sarova Lion Hill, Lake Nakuru National Park
11. Lake Nakuru
12. Tea Hotel, Kericho (Kipsigis)
13. Sunset Hotel, Kisumu, Lake Victoria
14. Kakamega National Reserve (Luhya)
15. Kericho (Luo)
16. Kisii Hotel, Kisii
17. Mara Serena Lodge, Maasai Mara National Reserve
18. Sarova Mara Camp, Maasai Mara National Reserve
19. Amboseli Serena Lodge, Amboseli National Park
20. Taita Hills Lodge, Chyulu Hills National Park (Maasai)
21. Mwatate, Tsavo National Park (Taita)
22. Mombasa (Giriama; Digo)
23. Nairobi National Park
24. The Ark, Aberdare National Park
25. Nyeri
26. Outspan, Aberdare National Park
27. Isiolo
28. Safariland Lodge, Lake Naivasha
29. Cottar's Camp, Maasai Mara National Reserve (Akamba)
30. Safari Park, Nairobi
31. Kabernet, Changarani Hills
32. Safari Park Lodge, Maralal

Locations are numbered in the order in which I visited them. The ethnic groups I contacted for stories are in italics.

Stories from the Kikuyu

Who Are the Kikuyu?

A long time ago, in the beginning, Mogai, Divider of the Universe, called the first man, Gikuyu, to Kere-Nyaga, *the Mountain of Brightness. He gave Gikuyu the land rich with trees and rivers and commanded him to build his home near a spot of fig trees,* mikoyo. *Mogai, also known as Ngai, provided Gikuyu with a beautiful wife, Moombi, the first woman. Together, they produced nine daughters, and, after a sacrifice of a lamb and a kid, Mogai presented each of the daughters with a husband. From these couples came the original clans of the Kikuyu people, and their home,* Mugurue wa Gathanga, *on the Mountain of Brightness (Mt. Kenya) remains sacred to these people, as does the fig tree.*

So begins the creation myth of the Kikuyu people of long ago. The influences of a modern lifestyle and a Christian education have replaced many of these traditional beliefs, but an understanding of who they were when the stories began is necessary to understand who they are today.

The center of traditional Kikuyu life was *nyomba* or *mbari*, the family group. Other governing principles were the clan, *moherega*, consisting of several *mbari* units who had the same clan name and were descended from the same family group, and the system of age grading, *riika*, which bonded boys and girls after initiation. It was a patriarchal system, although legends of long ago said that it was the women who originally dominated and ruled. After many generations, the men revolted during a time when the women were burdened with pregnancies; today the father is the head of the family and the custodian of the property.

Ownership of land is extremely important to the Kikuyu, for it is their way of life and part of their religion. Jomo Kenyatta, first president of independent Kenya and a member of the Kikuyu culture, wrote in his book *Facing Mount Kenya*:

It is the soil that feeds the child through a lifetime; and again after death it is the soil that nurses the spirits of the dead for eternity. Thus the earth is the most sacred thing above all that dwell in or on it. Among the Kikuyu the soil is especially honored, and an everlasting oath is to swear by the earth.

Men claimed ownership of land through inheritance and by growing crops on it, trapping wild animals, putting beehives in the trees, and grazing sheep, goats, and cattle on it. Men remained on their fathers' land, while women left their families to join their husbands. Fathers and male children were most important, for they assured that the family line, and the land, would not end. If a man died without a son, it was believed that the family group came to an end, and the ancestral spirits who looked after the family could no longer communicate with those still living.

Childhood was a time of learning, beginning with lullabies sung by the mother and nurse to teach infants the history and tradition of the family and clan. Once the child could speak, a game of asking questions about his or her ancestry would be played. Boys learned from their fathers about agriculture, trade, land, animals and plants, and identification of the family's herds through memorization of each cow, sheep, and goat. Girls learned their domestic duties of preparing foods, growing crops, and molding pottery. Both learned riddles, folklore, legends, and etiquette from their mothers and the elders.

Between the ages of ten and twelve for boys, and six to ten for girls, the Kikuyu passed out of childhood. The next stage of education included decision making, showing honor and respect to elders, obedience to parents, and understanding rights and responsibilities within the family and the clan. The final ceremony of initiation, *irua*, or circumcision, occurred at approximately age eighteen and allowed the adolescents to become full members of the clan.

Initiations were performed once a year for girls and every five or nine years for boys. Each age group, collectively, was given the name of an important event at the time of circumcision, thereby creating a way of recording and remembering history.

In *Facing Mount Kenya*, Kenyatta wrote about the circumcision of females (clitoridectomy) because of the concern expressed by Europeans and missionaries that the practice was barbaric and dangerous. He hoped that the ritual would be better understood through his descriptions of the precautions taken to avoid infections, as well as his explanations as to the significance of the ceremony. The procedure is briefly summarized here.

Preparation for female initiation included a special diet of beans and porridge to prevent loss of blood; instructions on the new lifestyle the girls would soon adopt; a blessing and anointing of the children with white chalk, *ira*, from Mt. Kenya; shaving their heads; a great ceremonial dance, *matuumo*; and a race to determine the leaders of both the male and female initiates. The morning of the clitoridectomy, the girls bathed until numb and then were operated on by a specialist trained since childhood. No display of fear or pain was acceptable. Afterward, the wound was sprinkled with milk and herbs, and the girls were taken to a special hut to sleep and heal.

On the eighth or twelfth day, after all were well following cleansing and treatments with medicines, the parents gathered for a ceremony of rebirth, symbolized by the cutting of a ribbon made from sheep gut, which represented the umbilical cord. The sheep's meat was eaten by everyone, and the initiates returned home. For the next three or four months they did no work but traveled around the district singing. At the end of that time they gathered for the final cleansing or purification, *menjo* or *gothiga*. Heads were shaved, old clothes were discarded, bodies were painted with red ochre and dressed in new clothes, and the girls were adorned with beads and amulets.

Although Kenyatta wrote few details about the corresponding ceremony for boys, he clearly stated that initiation was the most important custom among his people for both genders. "It is looked upon as a deciding factor in giving a boy or girl the status of manhood or womanhood in the Gikuyu community." He did explain that boys participated in *ira*, the anointing with white chalk, as well as *matuumo*, the great dance, followed by taking the tribal oath, *muuma wa anake*, when all initiates promised they would act as adults and would never reveal tribal secrets. Following the circumcision of the boys, they recovered under careful attendance by their parents, relatives, and friends. Like the girls, the boys spent several months traveling and singing throughout the district and attended the final purification ceremony of *menjo*.

Now there was more learning to be done. Young women were taught by their elders the customary ways to help their future husbands. They looked after the children, cooked, worked in the gardens, and preserved food. Young men practiced shooting with bow and arrows and fighting with a spear. They joined in cattle raids, and if they returned victorious, they sang songs of triumph and were given presents. They also spent their days building huts, clearing land, and learning how to defend the village against wild animals. They were now junior warriors, *njama ya anake*.

Marriage followed a long process of many months of negotiations and discussions between families, but it was a matter of choice, not arrangement. A young man and his friends would visit the girl who had caught his eye, and he would request "adoption." After several visits, she could indicate acceptance by telling him to speak with her parents. Then both sets of parents met over a ritual of beer drinking, followed by a series of visits from the prospective groom to give presents of sheep and goats or cattle to the bride's family. The engagement was announced through the public slaughter of a fat sheep.

The day of the wedding was chosen by the parents but kept secret from the bride. On the chosen day, she was "kidnapped" by the boy's female relatives, and she would stage a mock struggle with loud screaming and pleading for freedom. For eight days the girl was visited by other females of her age group, who sang songs of "mourning." The young couple was left alone at night to consummate the marriage. On the eighth day the bride was adopted into her husband's clan.

Duties for the husband and wife were clearly assigned by gender. The man tended the livestock, took care of any hard labor such as cutting trees, and was in charge of bee keeping, hunting, woodcarving, and smith work. The woman's responsibilities included all housework, the harvesting of crops, dressmaking, pottery, and weaving. The planting and weeding of crops was shared by both sexes.

Each woman had her own hut, *nyomba*, considered to be the traditional sacred place of the family, where communication with ancestral spirits could occur. The man's hut, *thingira*, was for visitors. When a new hut was needed, the community helped in collecting the building materials. The land was christened with sugarcane or honey beer, and the circular hut of wooden walls and grass-thatched roof was erected in one day, accompanied by much singing and followed by feasting. The ever-burning fire inside was lit in a ritual led by an elder accompanied by two children, male and female.

Inside *nyomba* were several partitions dividing the woman's bed, storage area, girls' bed, and areas for sheep and goats. The man's *thingira* had only one partition for his bed, and the rest was open as a sitting area. A well-built hut would last ten or more years, with thatching and wall repairs done by the women. Cow or sheep dung, which preserved the wood and prevented destruction from ants, was used to fill holes.

After a period of time, if the husband had enough wealth, he would marry again. Polygamy was acceptable for several reasons: 1) it provided greater assurance that children, especially sons, would inherit the land and continue the family; 2) children were a sign of prosperity and wealth; 3) it gave the man a chance to prove his ability to manage a household, thereby giving him the necessary status to become a respected elder of the clan; 4) wives desired help with their duties and chores; and 5) it indicated fondness for family. Having children was all-important; barrenness or impotence was a disgrace. Having several wives increased the size of a man's family, his land, and his wealth.

Wealth for a Kikuyu family was determined by ownership of cattle. Cows were "money in the bank." They were never eaten, except at times of famine. A very rich family might eat a bull or ox, or sacrifice one in a ceremony as a substitute for a goat or ram. Cow's milk was used only by the wealthy. Sheep and goats were used as the standard currency, for religious sacrifices, and as the chief source of meat, hides, and the necessary betrothal gifts.

Five principal councils governed the Kikuyu. Young men first became members of the junior warriors, *njama ya anake*, described earlier. After eighty-two months, they joined the senior warriors, *njama ya ita*, or war council. This group provided the defense and military force of long ago and was virtually eliminated when the British government prohibited free movement and raids between tribes. The other three councils collectively comprised the council of elders, *kiama*. Men entered the council as learners and messengers, *kiama kia kamatimo*. Upon circumcision of a man's first child, he became a member of the council of peace, *kiama kia mataathi*. When all of his children had been circumcised and his wives could no longer give birth, he became a member of the religious and sacrificial council, *kiama kia maturangugu*. These were the "holy men."

It was the council of elders, all three stages, who listened to complaints, settled disputes, and administered justice. All members could speak their ideas and recommendations; bribery was avoided through the practice of taking sacred and binding oaths. Serious crimes, such as murder, carried a predetermined fine of a certain number of sheep and goats. Adultery and rape also brought the even more feared punishment of ostracism from the clan.

Life for the Kikuyu of long ago was filled with hard labor and obtaining the necessary knowledge of survival skills. But there was time for play, too. Stories were told by mothers and grandmothers when the work was done. *Gicandi* songs were performed by traveling minstrels, who accompanied themselves with gourd rattles decorated with symbols recording their travels. Music was played at ceremonies with a variety of instruments: *kihembe*, a drum made from a hollowed-out tree trunk over which a skin is stretched; *njingiri*, small rattles worn around the ankles by dancers; *kegamba*, a large rattle worn under the knee; and *motoriro*, a bamboo flute played by men for leisure.

The religion of the Kikuyu was based on a firm belief in Ngai, the Creator, and a deep respect for all of nature, especially the land. Ngai manifested himself in the sun, moon, stars, and rainbows. Thunder was believed to be the cracking of his joints, and lightning was his sword. He rested on Mt. Kenya and was addressed only at times of great importance, such as birth, initiation, marriage, and death. Other personal crises or broken taboos required communication with ancestral spirits through a medicine man, *mondo-mogo*, who would determine the cause of their anger. Gifts of beer and a sacrificial lamb would be offered to appease the spirits.

Illness was often attributed to the anger of these spirits, too, especially if it followed an unresolved quarrel. Medicines would be used first, but if the illness continued, communication with the dead ancestors would ensue, and, if necessary, a sacrifice to Ngai would be performed. Other sacrificial ceremonies were

A fly whisk.

Who Are the Kikuyu?

held to request rain; they also took place at the planting, purifying, and harvesting of the crops.

A select group of elders among the Kikuyu were considered to be seers, or wise men, *athuri a kiama*. They had unusual powers that allowed them to communicate directly with Ngai. However, this power was a delicate one; any prophecy that proved false was a sentence of death for the seer. There were also those who could perform magic—create protective charms, cause someone to fall in love, bring fertility to a barren woman. But any magic that placed self ahead of family or community was intolerable; such destructive magic was witchcraft, and the convicted witch doctor would be sentenced to death by fire.

Like the rest of Kenya's people, the Kikuyu lived a life rich in tradition. Their intricate rites of passage and division of duties trained a society that respected the importance of each member's role in the clan's survival. But in the 1890s a great Kikuyu medicine man, Mogo wa Kebiro, predicted great changes for his people. He foresaw an iron snake that would spit fire and cross the land from east to west. He spoke of the arrival of strangers with skin that resembled a light-colored frog, and of a disease that would destroy the cattle. Before long, the railroad stretched across Kenya, opening the country to settlement by Europeans, the doctrines of Christian missionaries, and the demands of the British government. Herds of cattle were eliminated by rinderpest. The resulting turmoil eventually led to the violence of the Mau Mau revolt in the mid-1900s. While in forced exile from his people, Jomo Kenyatta wrote in *Facing Mount Kenya* of the several misunderstandings that had contributed to this conflict between the Kikuyu and the British.

First, the Kikuyu offered land to the new settlers as a sign of friendship and trust, not understanding that its removal from them was permanent. Second, the African ties of family were binding, and all generations, both living and dead, formed the family groups. The family could not be broken, nor could the ownership of the land, because it passed from father to son. Third, the Europeans valued an education based on the examination and testing of knowledge. The Kikuyu valued an education that emphasized experience and personal relations. And finally, the Kikuyu government was based on a progression from the family unit to the village council, composed of the heads of several families, to a district council of all the elders, to a national council chosen from the district council and having an elected president. There were no inheritable or appointed positions; advancement depended on an elder's merit. Well-established rules of conduct prohibited individualism, and a selfish man had no name or reputation in the community. The British government's practice of appointing "chiefs" to represent the Kikuyu was contrary to the clans' traditions of participation and elevation of status through appropriate behavior.

After nine years, Kenyatta was released by the British government. The Kikuyu proudly remember that one of their members was Mzee, President

Kenyatta, whose motto was *"Harambee,"* unity, and who helped to lead Kenya toward independence.

The Kikuyu of today are the largest ethnic group in Kenya. Their culture has changed in many ways, adapting to the needs of a modern society. The strong work ethic they established long ago as traders continues today in their labors as farmers and craftspeople. They are predominantly an agricultural society, growing cash crops of coffee, pyrethrum, vegetables, and flowers. They also make pottery from *riumba*, a clay found in their district, and *kiondo*, baskets woven from sisal and other fibers. They are blacksmiths, teachers, safari guides, and businesspeople.

Many of the rituals and ceremonies are no longer practiced as the people grow up in towns, are educated in schools, and lose their family ties. The Kikuyu are representative of a changing Kenya, a society of old traditions and new adaptations.

From My Journal

Naro Moru River Lodge, Mt. Kenya National Park

I am writing on the banks of Naro Moru River at the base camp for climbing Mt. Kenya.[1] The mountain is spectacular, rising 17,000 feet out of the mist and clouds. I first saw it at sunrise at Treetops Lodge as the cape buffalo silently appeared in single file from out of the forest. Baboons, "the roosters of Kenya," hooted as the sun rose, the elephants returned to the forests, and the buffalo came down to drink.

Ph.1. Base camp for climbing Mt. Kenya.

We have spent the morning collecting stories from two Kikuyu families. They were delighted to share their stories, and, one by one, daughters and sons joined in. Kagathi, my guide, translator, and friend, does a marvelous job of interpreting, enacting the animals and giggling when amused by a twist of events.

At the first house, Lucy, a shy girl of about six, had heard I was coming (her father, Timothy, is a friend of Kagathi's),[2] and she practiced her story all morning. But when I arrived, her mouth dropped open and she was frozen, too timid to say a word. So Kagathi gently guided her away so she could not see me, and she told him her story about Rabbit and the wizard.

I gave Kennedy, the boy who told "The Boy Who Went to Heaven," a toy horn. When we drove away, about an hour later, he stood on the edge of the road, horn in his hand, waving and yelling, *"Asante!"* (Thank you!) I waved and yelled back the same.

At the second home, they had all gathered in preparation for our arrival. The *mzee* (elder) sat in his chair, the *mama* (woman) next to him on the ground,[3] two daughters beside her and three babies crawling over legs and between arms. The grandmother had bare feet with bottoms like leather, a wonderful smile that revealed many missing or protruding teeth, and the traditional earlobes with huge holes. I loved her singing. One of her daughters told a

Ph.2. Kagathi (center) and Timothy (left).

clever story about the trickster, Rabbit, and I heard similarities with a Bre'r Rabbit story I tell.[4]

As the stories continued, more family members quietly joined us in the cornfield. I believe they were curious about *mama mzungu* (white woman), but I also believe they wanted to hear the stories. The stories are generally told at night or on Sundays, when the work is done.

Ph.3. The *mzee*, seated in a chair; the *mama*, seated next to him on the ground.

Ph.4. The woman on the left, holding the baby, told me
the story of "Rabbit and Lion."

July 4, 1988

Naro Moru River Lodge

Today, a year and a half later, I revisited Timothy's family at their home in Naro Moru.[5] Esther, his wife, welcomed us into an immaculate two-room house, a flowered cloth on the table, flowered wallpaper covering the cupboards, and flowered doilies on the old sofa. Esther fixed us *chai* (tea), thick with milk, while her children told stories.

Lucy is still shy, her whispery voice barely audible and her eyes fixed on her twisting hands. But she stayed with me. She got very flustered when the adults laughed uproariously at her story of Vulture, who is covered by Hyena's diarrhea. Her young innocence was in such contrast with the bawdiness of the tale. After she finished, she came to sit between Susan and me, obviously relieved not to be the center of attention any longer.

Kennedy, on the other hand, was eager to tell stories, quickly moving to the storyteller's stool placed in the middle of the room. The stories went on for almost two hours. When I thanked Esther for her family's wonderful stories, she said, "Oh, ever since you were here last time, the children have been telling stories."

I wish I could have taken Lucy home with me and taught her self-esteem. I wish I could give clever Kennedy the education he deserves. I wish I could believe that their stories will continue to be told long after I am gone. But everywhere I have gone, last year and this, they say, "I used to know so many stories, but now they are gone."

Ph.5. Timothy's family. My arm is around Kennedy, and Lucy is in front of me. Esther is the woman second from the left. (Photo courtesy of Susan Grant Raymond.)

The Boy Who Went to Heaven

Retold by Heather McNeil

There was once a boy who was told to look after his father's cattle. But the boy got busy carving a flute, or maybe he was chasing the wind, or maybe he just fell asleep. The cattle wandered into somebody else's garden.

When the boy discovered what had happened, he was filled with shame. When his father discovered what had happened, he was filled with anger. The boy was punished and sent home to his mother. And when his mother asked her son what had happened, he told her he wanted to go to heaven.

"Heaven," said the boy, "will be *mzuri*, beautiful." So his mother cooked him *ugali*. He put the porridge in *buyu*, a gourd, tied the gourd at his side, and walked down the road, *pole pole*, ever so slowly, looking for heaven.

As he walked down the road, he met a guard who asked the boy, "*Unakwenda wapi?* Where are you going?"

"I am going to heaven, because in heaven everything will be *mzuri sana*, very beautiful."

"Will you do me a favor?" asked the guard. "Will you turn my cows around and make them come this way?"

"*Ndiyo*, yes," said the boy. "I will try." So he followed the guard's directions and found not cattle, but *tembo wawili*, two cow elephants, huge and stubborn. The boy pushed and pulled and sang and whistled until, at last, the elephants turned around and walked back to the guard.

"*Asante sana*," said the guard. "Thank you very much."

"*Si kitu*," answered the boy. "You are welcome." And then he walked, *pole pole*, ever so slowly, down the road to heaven.

The boy met another guard. "*Unakwenda wapi?*"

"I am going to heaven," answered the boy, "because in heaven everything will be *mzuri sana*."

"Will you do me a favor? Will you turn my cows around?"

"*Ndiyo*, I will try." But when he followed the guard's directions, he found not cattle, not elephants, but *chui wawili*, two leopards, lean and hungry. The boy danced and jumped and petted and scratched, until, at last, the leopards turned around and walked back to the guard.

"*Asante sana*," said the guard.

"*Si kitu*," answered the boy. And then he walked, *pole pole*, ever so slowly, down the road to heaven.

The boy walked on until he came to *nyumba*, a house. "*Hodi?*" called the boy. "May I come in?" There was no answer. The boy could smell food, and he was hungry, for his mother's *ugali* had been eaten long ago.

"*Hodi?*" asked the boy again. He waited to hear "*Karibu!* You are welcome!" But there was still no answer. The boy's stomach grumbled and rumbled at the smell of maize and beans and meat cooking. But the boy did not go inside. Instead, he walked, *pole pole*, ever so slowly, down the road to heaven.

Finally, the boy arrived at the entrance to heaven. God's wife gave him food and water and showed him where to sleep. As the boy closed his eyes, God's wife said, "When you hear thunder, do not be afraid. It is only God coming home."

All night thunder boomed, but the boy slept soundly.

In the morning God asked to see His wife's visitor. The boy walked *pole pole*, ever so slowly, and bowed his head in front of God.

"*Karibu*," said God. "Tell me, what did you see as you walked the road to heaven?"

The boy thought about his long journey. "I saw a guard who asked me to turn his elephants around."

"And did you?" asked God.

"*Ndiyo*."

"*Nafahamu*. I understand. And what else did you see as you walked the road to heaven?"

"I saw a second guard who asked me to turn his leopards around."

"And did you?"

"*Ndiyo*."

"*Nafahamu*. And what else did you see as you walked the road to heaven?"

"I saw *nyumba* and I smelled food cooking. I called out '*Hodi*?' but nobody answered '*Karibu!*' "

"And did you go inside and eat?"

"*La!* No!"

"*Nafahamu*. And now I shall reward you for what you have done on the road to heaven. Pull up this clump of grass."

The boy pulled and pulled and pulled, and out of the hole where the grass once grew came *ng'ombe wingi sana*, so many cattle.

God said, "Now, pull up this clump of grass." The boy pulled and pulled and pulled, and out of the hole where the grass once grew came *kondoo na mbuzi wingi sana*, so many sheep and goats.

The boy went home, and he was rich.

Now this boy had a brother, and when this brother saw all the cattle, sheep, and goats his brother owned, he wanted such richness for himself. He was jealous, and he was greedy. So he told his mother to prepare *ugali* for him. He put the porridge into *buyu*, tied it to his side, and began to walk down the road to heaven. But this boy did not walk *pole pole*, ever so slowly. He walked *haraka haraka*, quicker and quicker. Very soon he met the first guard.

"*Unakwenda wapi?*"

"I am going to heaven so I will be rich."

"Will you do me a favor? Will you turn my cows around?"

"*La!* I am in a hurry." And the boy walked on, *haraka haraka*, quicker and quicker, down the road to heaven.

He met the second guard. When he was asked to turn the cows around, again he answered, "*La!* I am in a hurry." And the boy walked on, *haraka haraka*, quicker and quicker, down the road to heaven.

When he came to the empty house, he smelled the maize and the beans and the meat cooking. He did not call out "*Hodi?*" He did not wait to hear "*Karibu!*" He entered *nyumba*, and he ate until his stomach was full and tight as a drum. Then he walked on, *haraka haraka*, quicker and quicker, until, finally, he came to heaven.

God's wife gave him food and water and showed him where to sleep. She said, "If you hear thunder, do not wake up. It is only God on His way home." But all night the boy lay awake listening to the thunder, anxious to get his reward.

In the morning God asked to see His visitor. The brother walked *haraka haraka*, quicker and quicker, with his head held high.

"*Karibu*," said God. "Tell me, what did you see as you walked the road to heaven?"

The boy answered with impatience. "I saw a guard who asked me to turn his cows around."

"And did you?"

"*La!* I was in a hurry."

"*Nafahamu*. And what else did you see as you walked the road to heaven?"

"I saw another guard who asked me to turn his cows around."

"And did you?"

"*La!* I was in a hurry."

"*Nafahamu*. And what else did you see as you walked the road to heaven?"

"I saw *nyumba*, and I smelled food cooking."

"And did you go inside and eat the food?"

"*Ndiyo*. I was hungry."

"*Nafahamu*. And now I shall reward you for all that you have done on the road to heaven. Pull up this clump of grass and you will find your reward."

The boy quickly reached out and grabbed the clump of grass. As he pulled, he thought of *ng'ombe na kondoo na mbuzi wingi sana*, so many cows and sheep and goats that would soon be his. As he pulled, he thought of how he would soon be as rich as his brother. As he pulled, he thought about how he could get more from God.

The boy pulled and pulled and pulled, until, from out of the hole where the grass once grew, came *chui*, the leopard, lean and hungry. And the leopard ate the brother.

The Boy Who Went to Heaven

Original Translation

There was one little boy. That boy was looking after the cattle, and he let the cattle go into somebody's garden. When the father came (it was somebody else's garden, so he came to the father), so he got the father, and they beat him (the boy) very well. Then the boy was very mad, and he talked to the mother and told the mother he just wanted to go to heaven. Then the mother cooked some food. Then he got the food in a little bag and just went.

So when he was walking, he came upon another guard looking after the cattle. He asked the boy, "Where are you going?"

The boy said, "I just want to go to heaven."

The guard said, "Can you just do me a favor?"

The boy said, "What? Yes, I can do you a favor."

"Can you go and turn the cows to come this way?"

So the boy went and turned the cows back to the man. When the old man told the boy to turn the cows around, they weren't cows, they were elephants.

He continued. He walked and walked until he met another guard who was looking after the cattle. He told him the same thing, but this time they were leopards.

So he went. He came to a house in the bush and there was some food cooking in there. He didn't eat the food.

Then he went, and he met the Son of God. He entered this little house and he met God's wife. She had seven heads. They gave him food and somewhere to sleep. Then he was told, "When you hear the thunders, don't wake up. God will come by then." So the thunders were growling all night, and he didn't wake up.

So God came, and He said, "Oh, you have a visitor." She said, "Yes." Then she was told to call him to come and see. Then he was asked by God, "The road that you passed, what did you see on the way?"

He said, "I met two cow elephants. I was told by this man to go and turn them around. So I did. I met a leopard. I was told the same thing, and I did. Then I came and I met this house. There was some food cooking. There was nobody in there, but I didn't eat the food. Then I met the Son of God, and I said hello."

And he was asked, "When you entered this house, what did you see?"

"Nothing."

Then God told the wife, "Get the boy up in the morning, give him food and give him a lot to drink." Then he was told by God to pull a piece of grass out, and cattle came out all over the place, so many of them. Then he was told, "Pull the next one." And he pulled. Then some sheep and goats came out of the second hole. Then the boy was escorted by God with all his cattle and goats to his home. And when he got to his home, they had a cage already fixed for all his cows.

Then the other boy said to the father, "Father, come out and see all these cattle and sheep and goats." And the other boy, the second oldest, was jealous. So the second boy went and did the same. He went and looked after the cattle, and they grazed somebody's garden. Then he came and was beaten up, and he said the same thing, he just wanted to go to heaven. He was given the same treatment. He was given food. Then he started walking. Then he met the same man and was told to go and turn around the elephants. The same thing. Then he met the second one, he did the same thing. "Go and turn around the leopard." Then he went and turned it around and told the man he just wanted to go to heaven. He asked, "Can you show me the way?"

So when he entered the house of God, God came out and said the same thing, "Give this boy food and everything." In the morning, he woke up and was told to pull the grass, and a leopard came up and ate the boy.

Notes and Tips on the Telling

Notes

- The original telling did not make the second boy as arrogant as I do. However, it did not seem logical to me that the brother would be punished by God if the boy had helped the guards and not eaten the food. So I made him more obviously selfish, anxious only to reward himself with riches even though he did nothing worth rewarding.

- Kenya is a melting pot of cultures, including their various religions. The Son of God and a wife of God with seven heads in the same story was a confusing mixture to me. Research at the Iliff School of Theology in Denver gave me no clues as to the origins of the wife. The story was told to me by a young boy whose memory and imagination may be the origin. So I simplified the wife and eliminated the Son of God, because he played no part in the story.

- Kagathi, my guide, taught me a proverb I have remembered often as I rush through life's hectic schedules. This story seems a perfect example of its moral: "*Haraka haraka haina baraka.*" "Hurry hurry has no reward."

Tips

- Consider using audience participation with the repeated Swahili phrases. The first time, say the Swahili and the English translation. After that, make it apparent through your body language (head nod, hand gesture, etc.) that listeners are encouraged to join in. Repeat the phrase the same number of times so that your audience does not get confused as to what you expect. Also, you should not have to give the English translation each time, because it will be apparent through its place in the story what the word means.

- Some of my retellings in this collection do not require the use of Swahili, but this one does, for the rhythm. Use the glossary for correct pronunciation. Practice until you can say the words easily and correctly.

- The section of the story about the first boy should be told slowly, with care and precision. The portion about the second boy should be hurried, almost reckless. The listeners know the pattern already, but his selfish actions should be emphasized with a brief pause or change of speed and voice pattern. His conversation with God should *not* be hurried, setting the mood for God's decision to punish him.

- YOU MUST REMEMBER TO TELL EACH AND EVERY STORY IN YOUR OWN WORDS, AND IN A MANNER THAT IS COMFORTABLE TO YOU! Do not memorize the story exactly as it is printed. Read it over and over, many times over many days, allowing the story to "settle in." Read the original translation, too. Are you an auditory learner? Record the story and listen to it, over and over, as you're driving to work or while putting in miles on your exercise bike. Meanwhile, do your homework and research the people, their customs, the animals, their habits. Then begin creating your own version, using the basic plot and favorite phrases, but with your own talents and style. If the story sings to you, then you can give it life. Telling my story verbatim, in my words and in my style, means you don't trust yourself. If all you can do is copy, then it isn't meant to be your story.

Stories from the Kikuyu

Rabbit and Lion
Retold by Heather McNeil

Sungura the Rabbit[6] was singing—not because he was happy but because he was hungry. This was a time of drought, and all the animals were dying of hunger and thirst. Even clever Sungura could not find anything to eat, so he was trying to forget the pain and emptiness in his belly by singing.

Now, all the time that he was singing and dancing, he did not realize he was being watched. Hiding behind the bushes was Simba the Lion. He, too, had pain in his empty belly, and his mouth watered as Sungura danced closer and closer.

Lion watched.

Lion waited.

Lion crouched.[7]

All of a sudden Sungura found himself face to face, nose to nose, whisker to whisker with Simba!

"Eh, Rabbit! I am going to have to eat you now," said Lion.

Ph.6. Sungura the Rabbit.

Rabbit trembled with fear. "Eh, Lion! You go right ahead and eat me. It will give me great honor to (gulp) die inside your mouth. But it is too bad that before I (gulp) die, we will not share in *karamu*, the feast I was just planning."

"*Karamu*? What feast? There is no feast. There is only hunger. Even I, the great Simba, can capture only one scrawny rabbit. And that is why I am going to have to eat you."

Ph.7. Lion watched. Lion waited. Lion crouched.

"Yes, you already said that. But I really was planning a feast. Just now I was thinking about delicious *swala pala*, the impala. I was thinking about fat *punda milia*, the zebra. I was thinking about tasty *ngiri*, the warthog. But now we shall never find out if my plan for *karamu* would have worked, since I am going to (gulp) die."

"Eh, Rabbit. What is this plan of yours? Tell me, and if it is a good plan, perhaps you will live a bit longer."

So Sungura told Simba his plan.

Lion listened.

Lion smiled.

Lion laughed. From deep in his empty belly, he laughed.

"*Nzuri sana*. Well done, Rabbit. It is a good plan. And if the plan works, you shall share *karamu* with me."

"*Asante sana*, Simba. Thank you very much, Lion. And now you know what you must do?"

"I know what *you* must do, Sungura. You must dig me *shimo*, a hole."

"*I* must dig you *shimo*? You can just dig your own *shimo*, Lion. Huh!"

"Sungura," said Lion, taking one step closer and speaking very slowly, "you are indeed a very clever rabbit, but may I remind you that I am a very hungry LION!"

So Rabbit dug the hole. *Haraka haraka*, very quickly, he dug the hole for Lion. The hole was so deep that when Lion jumped down inside, all that remained above the ground were his ears. Then Lion tilted back his head, and Rabbit kicked all the red earth back into the hole, leaving only Lion's eyes and nose uncovered so he could see and breathe.

Then Rabbit put on *njingiri*, his ankle bells, picked up *ngoma*, his drum, and began to sing and dance through the bushes:

> Ho, ho, my eyes are seeing in the dirt.
> Ho, ho, my eyes are growing in the dirt.

Along came Ngiri the Warthog. "What are you saying, Sungura? Eyes cannot see in the dirt. Eyes see in the head."

But Rabbit did not answer Warthog. He just kept on singing and dancing, so Warthog followed along behind Rabbit to figure out why he was singing such a foolish song:

> Ho, ho, my eyes are seeing in the dirt.
> Ho, ho, my eyes are growing in the dirt.

Along came Swala Pala the Impala.[8] "Sungura, what is all this foolish noise you are making? Eyes do not grow in the dirt. Eyes grow in the head."

But Rabbit did not answer Impala. He kept on singing and dancing, so Impala followed along behind Warthog, behind Rabbit, to figure out why he was singing such a foolish song.

On and on danced Rabbit, and the farther he danced into the bushes, the more animals followed along behind. There was Twiga the Giraffe, Paa the Gazelle, and Mbogo the Buffalo. They all

Ph.8. Swala Pala the Impala.

Rabbit and Lion

asked Rabbit what he was singing about, but Rabbit ignored them all. They followed him into the bushes, out of the bushes, and then into a circle, a circle that grew smaller and smaller around a certain mound in the dirt.

Of course, under that mound of dirt was—Simba! The lion watched as the animals came closer and closer.

Lion waited.

Lion crouched.

Lion ROARED! The great Simba jumped out of the hole and grabbed a zebra here, a gazelle there, a warthog and an impala. He dragged them down into his hole and all the other animals ran away.

Except Rabbit. Sungura hopped over to the hole, looked down, and there inside sat Simba, happily gulping and smacking and swallowing. Sungura spoke very slowly.

"Eh, Simba! You are indeed a very hungry lion. But may I remind you that you are now filling up your belly because I am a very clever rabbit!"

Lion listened.

Lion smiled.

Lion laughed. From deep in his full belly, he laughed. Rabbit jumped down into the hole, and, together, Sungura and Simba feasted all day.

Original Translation

A long time ago there was a rabbit and a lion. They met somewhere in the bush. And the lion told the rabbit, "I have to eat you." The lion told the rabbit, "If I don't eat you, you have to dig me a hole." The rabbit dug the hole for the lion. The lion entered inside and was left with just the eyes sticking out, looking up. And the rabbit started walking, singing, "Ho, ho, ho, ho. My eyes are seeing in the dirt. My eyes are growing in the dirt." The other animals came. This was a trick so the other animals would come, and then the lion would just jump at once. So he started looking.

The rabbit knew what was happening, but the other animals didn't. The lion started looking at the fat one and jumped at the fat one. The lion came up and jumped on the fat one. The lion called to the rabbit to come and have feast with him.

Rabbit and Lion

Tips on the Telling

Tips

- This story works best with tension and humor. That's why I added the repetitions ("Lion watched. Lion waited ...," etc.) Take your time and use effective pauses. The humor can be established by remembering that Rabbit is a legendary trickster, who sounds simple and foolish, but acts sly and clever. Exaggerated gulps, sidelong glances, and smirks will bring your Rabbit to life.

- The Swahili and the English are interchangeable. Use whatever sounds best for the rhythm. Use the Swahili only if you are comfortable with it.

- Rabbit's song should repeat throughout the story. At the beginning, I use humming only, which repeats after each "Lion watched ..." When Rabbit is luring the other animals, I repeat a portion of the song again after each "Lion waited ..." Try different patterns and use what feels right. However, avoid too much repetition; three times is usually enough.

- Visit an import store and consider purchasing a musical instrument to accompany the song. I use a drum and ankle bells. You could also make a thumb piano, following the directions in *Make Mine Music!* by Tom Walther (1981) or those in *Making and Playing Musical Instruments* by Afke den Boer and Margot de Zeeuw (1989).

- Make up your own tune to match your instrument. Listen to recordings of East African music (available at your public library or folk music store) to get an idea of rhythm and melody. For information about Kenyan music, use *Folk Music of Kenya* by George W. Senoga-Zake (1986) and *Traditional Musical Instruments of Kenya* by P. N. Kavyu (1980).

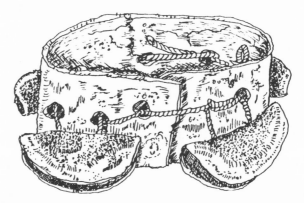

Njingiri—ankle bells.

Stories from the Turkana

Who Are the Turkana?

Legend says that the Turkana migrated into Kenya 200 to 300 years ago. Originally, they were Jie, one of the branches of the Karamojong tribe. But a new tribe was created when a group of young men followed a lost ox into the Korash Valley, where they found an old Jie woman gathering fruit in a country rich with berries. They persuaded others of the Jie to join them, and they gave themselves the name Turkana, perhaps derived from Turkwen, meaning "cave men," and invaded the Maasai's Embasso Narok (Black Lake) area, now known as Lake Turkana. Turkana rampages and cattle raids forced out the Pokot, Rendille, and Samburu people west of the lake. In the 1960s and 1970s, severe droughts forced the Turkana to wander again, this time in search of pastureland. Some have become farmers, a few are fishermen, but the majority are still nomadic herdsmen who follow the brief rains.

Most of the needs of the Turkana are met by their livestock. Cattle hides make sleeping mats, covers for huts, and sandals. Horns are used for snuff containers. Donkeys and camels are the pack animals. Goats and sheep, herded by the young boys, are killed for guests or minor rituals. Camels give milk for babies and are eaten when old or sick. Their hides are made into containers that are decorated with beads and cowrie shells and are used to hold butter, fat, and milk.

The main diet of the Turkana consists of meat, milk, and blood. When the latter is required, a tourniquet is put around the cow's neck to make the great veins stand out. An arrow is fired into the vein, and the blood is collected. The wound is then patched with mud and cow dung.

In preparation for the long dry seasons, *edodo* is made by boiling fresh milk, then drying it on skins. Wild berries are crushed and made into cakes or ground into dried meal. During famine the Turkana will eat fish. They are masters at the art of survival.

Perhaps in contrast to their harsh, dry, barren surroundings, the Turkana decorate themselves with brightly colored beads and elaborate hairstyles. The women wear layers of bead necklaces, brass or copper earrings, and sometimes a lip plug pierced through the lower lip. At ceremonies they wear beaded skirts and numerous necklaces of ostrich-egg beads and cowrie shells. Men twist their hair into small plaits, cover the braids with clay, and shape them into a bun on top of the head. Status is indicated by inserting ostrich feathers into holders of cow gut or macrame, which are then placed in the hair while the clay is still wet. It takes up to three days to complete the creation, which will last as long as three months. Men sleep with their heads propped on wooden saddlelike pillows so their hair will not be disturbed.

Age grades and initiations do not exist among the Turkana. Instead they name alternating generations the Leopards or the Stones. *Athapan*, the traditional passage into manhood, is achieved by killing an angry bull with a spear.

Before *athapan*, a boy carries only a piece of iron to defend himself and the livestock from hyenas. After *athapan*, his weapons are eight-foot spears, shields, bow and arrows, and a bludgeon. He also wears arm rings and finger rings of thin, sharp metal that slice and cut. The Turkana have been described as exceptionally fearless and the finest fighting men in East Africa.

Marriage is a three-year ceremonial process beginning with the kidnapping of the bride and ending with the weaning of the first child. Daily life consists of tending to the animals, preparing food, and growing a few crops such as millet and gourds. Crafts include working with leather, metal, bones, stones, wood, beads, seeds, shells, horns, tusks, and plumes.

Buyu—a gourd container.

Turkana religion is based on a belief in Akuji Nameri, the God of the Stars. The Turkana also believe in spirits, Nipen, and sacrifices of livestock are made to placate them when accidents, famine, or epidemics occur.

Perhaps what distinguishes the Turkana most is their amazing adaptation to their physical surroundings. For hundreds of years they have survived in a land of heat and sand. But now settlements and farms invade their territory, and they are no longer separated from modern lifestyles. The Turkana homeland is changing, and their unique customs, traditions, and stories are at risk.

From My Journal

July 18, 1988

Lake Baringo Lodge

It has been an incredible day of stories and sun. Kagathi arranged for us to visit a Turkana family in Baringo. The grandson, Harry, remembered me from last year. He's very intelligent and speaks excellent English, but Kagathi said he's decided to quit school now that he's finished level eight (about age fourteen). He took us to his home to hear stories from his grandmother, and what a show she gave us!

We sat outside on wooden stools that were each covered with a fluorescent green yarn doily. The grandmother and her two female friends sat on a grass mat, singing and clapping a song of welcome.[9] The first few stories were told all the way through in Turkana, then Harry translated from Turkana into Swahili, and Kagathi translated into English. The women giggled and punched each other, one sometimes interrupting and taking over the story from another. They *enjoyed* telling stories! The stories were rambling and rather anticlimactic, but the acompanying rituals of finger snapping, chanting, and hand clapping were wonderful. There was one especially intricate technique of snapping a finger of one hand over the back of a finger on the other hand to give emphasis during repetition.

Ph.9. The Turkana grandmother and her two friends welcomed me. (Photo courtesy of Susan Grant Raymond.)

The women were very different from each other. One was dressed in traditional *kangas,* cloths wrapped and draped around women, with layers of Turkana beads around her neck and six large silver hoops pierced through the left ear. The others wore modern dresses and beads. Harry's grandmother had a knit cap on her bald head and only a few teeth left in her mouth. Her skin was as wrinkled as the skin of a passion fruit, and Harry's toddler sister poked and pinched at her grandmother's arm, obviously fascinated by its parchmentlike texture.

Harry's father told a true story about a meat thief, portraying the thief hiding in trees and stepping over sleeping bodies. He often used as a prop a door that was stuck in the middle of the yard, attached to nothing and serving no purpose that I could see.

Harry's mother also told a story, one very similar to the Taita story I heard last year of "Rabbit and the Well." In her version it is Tortoise who manages to capture Rabbit. The mother was a round-faced beauty, quietly nursing her infant and looking too young to have another son fourteen years old.

When we left, Harry was visibly disappointed. I imagine he had hopes of traveling with us, maybe even coming back to the United States with me. It is always very difficult for me to leave.

Next, we headed out on a long, hot, slow ride to Kapendo, driving *pole pole* over the rocks and through the streams. We saw camels, goats, and an occasional Turkana herdsman. In the very remote and arid town of Kinyangi, Kagathi bartered on my behalf for the privilege of taking pictures. Sometimes it was 10 shillings ($.50) sometimes 20 ($1). One group of handsome Pokot men, complete with blue clay skullcaps, pompons on one side of the head, and spears and headrests in their hands, demanded 1,000 shillings ($50). I declined.

We stopped for a Schweppes in a very hot, very crowded general store in Kinyangi. Pokot and Turkana men and women were buying maize, beads, and sodas. The store was run by Somalis, the woman sluggish with weight but still bearing the dark-eyed beauty of those women. Kagathi said, "You can be in the most remote part of Kenya, and the shops will always be owned by Somalis or Indians. They get very rich." Kikuyu are the farmers; Akamba are the craftsmen; Maasai, Samburu, and Turkana are the herdsmen. The women of all tribes are the laborers.

Stories from the Turkana

Not So!

Retold by Heather McNeil

A long time ago, nobody ever listened to Ground Squirrel. Now, Ground Squirrel was *mdogo sana*, very small. But he was also *akili sana*, very clever. His name was Kidiri, and this is his story.

There came a time when Mama Simba,[10] the mother of the lions, had two babies, *watoto wawili*.[11] Oh, she was so proud! She took her babies to the water hole, and all day she bragged about how her babies would be the handsomest, the fastest, the strongest of all the animals.

Ph.10. Mama Simba.

Mama Nyani, the mother of the baboons, heard all the bragging, and she was not impressed. She gathered her own two babies onto her back, where she knew they would be safe.[12] Then she climbed up into a tree and called down to the lion, "Hey, Mama Simba! What makes you think your babies are so special? Look at them! What can they do? They growl like frogs, they sleep like lazy hyenas, and they fall over their own feet like clumsy beetles!"

Ph.11. Two lion cubs.

When the animals heard this, they laughed and laughed—except for Mama Simba. The mother of the lions did not laugh, and the mother of the lions did not forget.

Later that day, Mama Nyani went down to the water hole to get a drink of *maji*, water. While she was gone, her babies played roll-and-tumble and hide-and-jump and catch-a-tail. And all the time that they were playing, they did not realize they were being watched. Hiding in the bushes was Mama Simba. She waited until the baby baboons came rolling and tumbling by, and then—THWACK! THWACK!—she held a baby baboon under each of her front paws. Oh, such a screeching and hollering they made, and that brought Mama Nyani running back from the water hole.

"*Watoto wangu!* My babies! Let my babies go!"

"What are you talking about, Mama Nyani? These are not your babies. These are my babies."

Ph.12. Mama Nyani, the mother of the baboons.

"What are *you* talking about, Mama Simba? How could they be your babies?"

"They are with me, are they not? So they must be mine."

"Those babies have thick, brown fur, the color of mud. You have fur the color of grass. Those babies have arms like vines so they can swing in the trees. You do not swing in the trees. Those babies have hands like human hands. You have the paws, the claws, the fangs of a cat. Let my babies go!"

"Very well, Mama Nyani. I will let these babies go if there is one animal here who will stand in front of me, look into *macho yangu*, my eyes, and say these are not my children. Which one of you animals will say this to me?"

Nyamaza. Silence. There was not one animal who would walk up to the mother of the lions, look into her eyes, and call her a liar. Except Kidiri! The little ground squirrel knew the babies belonged to Mama Nyani, so he called out, "Not so! Not so! It is not so!"

But, as usual, no one heard Kidiri.

So he puffed out his chest, and a little bit louder he called out, "Not so! Not so! It is not so!"

Still, no one heard Kidiri.

The little ground squirrel stood up tall on his toes, puffed out his chest, and yelled as loud as he could, "NOT SO! NOT SO! IT IS NOT SO!"

But still, no one heard Kidiri.

So now he ran—plippity, plippity, plip—over to Mama Nyani and began to pull on her leg. The mother of the baboons looked down and, very annoyed, cried, "Hey, Kidiri! What are you doing? What do you want?"

The little ground squirrel stood up tall, puffed out his chest, and called out, "Not so! Not so! It is not so!"

"What's that?" said Mama Nyani. "What did you say?"

"Not so! Not so! It is not so!"

"Oh, *rafiki mdogo wangu!* My little friend! You must say that to Mama Simba!"

"But she will not hear me. And I'm not going to pull on her leg! But I have an idea. You and the other baboons must build me a tall mound of dirt, so tall that when I stand on the top, I can look into *macho ya simba*, the eyes of the lion. Then you must dig *shimo*, a hole, all the way down the middle of the mound of dirt and into the earth below."

So Mama Nyani called together all the baboons, and, with their hands like human hands, they built the mound of dirt. Then they dug *shimo* down through the middle of the mound and into the earth below.

Kidiri climbed to the top of the mound of dirt, looked directly into *macho ya simba*, and called out, "Not so! Not so! It is not so!"

"*What* did you say, Kidiri?"

The little ground squirrel gulped with fear. "Not so? Not so! It is not so! Those babies with dark brown fur, those babies with arms like vines, those babies with hands like human hands, those are the babies of Mama Nyani!" And—PLIP!—Kidiri disappeared down into the hole.

"RAAWR!" Mama Simba leaped forward to grab the ground squirrel, and as she did so, she lifted up her front paws, and—WHISH!—the two baby baboons ran back to their mother. But the mother of the lions

 was not going to let the ground squirrel get away, too. With her paw, she reached down into the hole, but she could not reach far enough. So she called for Tembo, the Elephant, and, using his trunk, Tembo reached down, down, down into the hole until his trunk wrapped around the leg of Kidiri.

Kidiri could feel himself being pulled back up the hole toward the angry lion, but, remember, he was not only *mdogo sana*, he was also *akili sana*. Kidiri called out, "Oh, silly Tembo. You think you are pulling my leg? You are not pulling my leg. You are pulling ... you are pulling ... you are pulling the root of a tree!"

So Tembo let go of what he thought was the root of a tree, and he felt all around with his trunk until it wrapped around ... the root of a tree! And while Tembo pulled and pulled on what he thought was the leg of the ground squirrel, and while Mama Simba paced and paced in front of the mound of dirt waiting for the little ground squirrel to appear, Kidiri dug his way through to his tunnels in the earth, and he ran away, laughing and saying, "Not so! Not so! It is not so!"

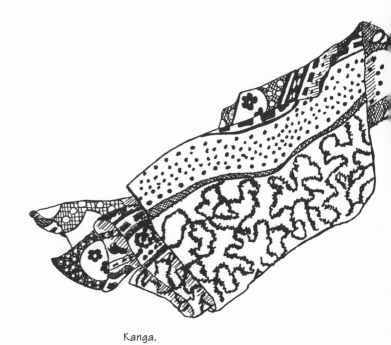

Kanga.

Original Translation (Turkana)

One time the lion had three cubs, but they were very ugly. The ostrich had her young ones, very beautiful. When the ostrich was away in the forest feeding, the lion came and stole the chicks and put her cubs where the ostrich was. When the ostrich came, she found the lion cubs. The ostrich went to the forest and called all the animals. They came and sat down. There was a discussion as to who stole whose young ones, but all the animals were scared of the lion, so they wouldn't say anything.

Then the ground squirrel said, "Me, I'm very short. Even if I talk, you wouldn't hear what I was talking about, because my voice is very small, too. Find me a tall termite mound, and I'll stand up there so you can hear what I'm talking about."

So they found this tall termite mound, and he climbed up to the top. Then he started addressing the animals: "The cubs belong to the lion, and the chicks belong to the ostrich."

When the lion heard that, he got mad. He went after the squirrel, but the squirrel went into the hole.

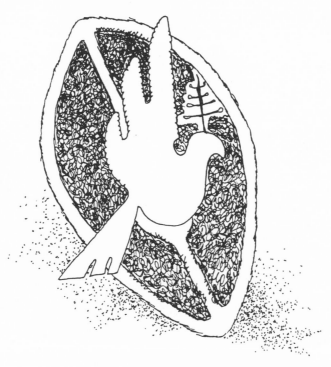

A dove on a war shield—symbol of President Kenyatta's efforts at peace and unity.

Original Translation (Samburu)

The lion had cubs, and the baboon had young ones, too. The lion cubs got sick. The lion saw that the baboon's young ones were not sick, so he decided to go and take away the baboon's young ones.

All the animals started calling one another. They decided to have a big meeting. All the animals, since they feared the lion, would come out and say, "Yes, we know those young ones belong to the lion."

Then the ground squirrel was very bold. He came and stood up and said, "Yes, I know all those young ones belong to the baboon." Then he got worried and told all the other animals, "Build a big mountain with a hole in the top. I'll climb up there and talk to all the other animals."

The ground squirrel said, "These young ones belong to baboon!" After talking, he got in that hole.

The lion ran to the elephant. He told the elephant, since he is the one with the long arm, "Take this ground squirrel for me."

The elephant got his trunk inside. He grabbed the squirrel's leg. The squirrel said, "Oh, you have just grabbed the root of a tree, not my leg." The elephant left the leg and grabbed the root of a tree. The squirrel cried, "Oh, you are breaking my leg, you are breaking my leg, you are breaking my leg!" when he was just grabbing the root.

Then the squirrel went into another of his holes, came out, and ran away. That is why, you see, even today, the ground squirrel stays in his hole, and the lion does not have young ones with thick fur and feet like humans.

Notes and Tips on the Telling

Notes

- There are published versions of this story. Be sure to read *Lion and the Ostrich Chicks* by Ashley Bryan (1986).

- I actually heard several different versions of this story. Sometimes it was mongoose, sometimes ground squirrel, sometimes baboon, sometimes ostrich.

Tips

- Visit a zoo. Watch these animals, how they walk, eat, turn their heads, communicate. It will make a difference in your telling.

- This is a perfect story for using different voices to match the different temperaments of the animals, if you are comfortable doing so. Baboon, often the evil pest in Kenyan folktales, is brazen and loud. Lion is strong and self-assured and has all the time in the world. Ground Squirrel, like the trickster Rabbit, is small, nervous, and clever out of necessity. Each animal's characteristics should be apparent in your interpretation, with different voices and body movements. However, be cautious of too much exaggeration and too many acrobatics. Keep your movements controlled and your voices believable. Rely on what I call a "sympathetic audience" (friend, spouse, fellow storyteller) to let you know whether you have surpassed reality and entered the world of the overly dramatic.

- Invite the audience to participate in the many repetitions of "Not so! Not so! It is not so!" Do it alone the first two times; a simple nod and hand gesture will invite the listeners to join in on the third refrain and every time after that. Children need very little encouragement; adults need "permission" to join in the telling before you begin.

Stories from the Akamba

Who Are the Akamba?

It was Usuu the Grandmother who told the stories in the evenings of long ago. She told how their god, Mulungu, put the first man and woman on Mount Nzaui. They were joined by another couple from the center of the earth. Mulungu sent rain, made the land fertile, and life began.

Long ago, the traditions and rituals of the Akamba began at birth, when the child would be named after a grandparent or an event that occurred at the time of birth. A boy born at night would be named Mutuka; a girl, Nduku. A boy born during a rainstorm would be called Wambua; a girl, Mumbua.

Children spent their days looking after the goats and calves and learning about trees and plants so their livestock would come home well fed and the firewood they collected would be useful. The ritual of circumcision, performed for both girls and boys at approximately the age of twelve, marked the end of childhood. During adolescence, girls worked with their mothers, learning household duties. Boys were encouraged to spend time with the elders, learning the skills of iron working, arrow making, and bee keeping. Men would also teach through stories, riddles, and proverbs told at sunset around a fire.

A second ceremony heralded the transition from adolescence to adulthood. Boys and girls were separated, and they spent a week with chosen elders called *avwikii*, who taught them about growing up. At the end of the week, a boy's ability to defend his family and the clan was tested. Someone wearing rhinoceros skins and making frightening noises would suddenly charge him. If the boy was scared and ran away, he was regarded as a coward and a misfit. But if the boy was brave and tried to shoot the animal, he passed the test. Those who passed the various tests designed to prove their knowledge and courage were considered adult and permitted to marry.

A young man was allowed to marry a girl of his own choosing; a girl could reject her suitor's proposal by simply returning the two goats he was required to give to the bride's household. Throughout courtship, several meetings were held between the families in order to strengthen ties, and a proper wedding required the blessings of the bride's father. The bridewealth, paid by the groom, was an amount agreed upon by the two families. Its purpose was much like that of a marriage certificate, and payment to the bride's family sometimes lasted a lifetime. If the marriage proved to be unsuccessful and a divorce was granted by the council of elders, the bridewealth was returned.

After the wedding, the woman left her parents and went to live with her husband and his family. The Akamba lived in large homesteads of family and friends. If a man had more than one wife, each wife built her own house of wood and grass or clay with thatched roofs. Houses were circular, with a central pole supporting the roof and providing a place to hang valuables. At the foot of the pole was the fire pit for cooking.

Adulthood was divided into distinct stages, each signifying increasing responsibility and wisdom. Young fathers constructed and maintained fences, built houses, and dug plots for gardening. Until a man's children were ready for circumcision, he was considered *mwanake*, a junior elder. Young mothers were responsible for cooking, fetching water and wood, gardening, and home repairs. A woman at this stage of life was called *mwiitu*. When a couple's children became junior elders, the father announced his retirement as *mwanake* with a ceremonial party, *kukula*. After this ritual, he was *nthele*, medium elder, with more responsibility and the possibility of being selected by the senior elders to be a chief, *munene*. If chosen to hold this position, he would meet strangers to determine whether they were harmful, and he would help administer the law. The senior elders also selected a council, *king'ole*, that dealt with criminal cases.

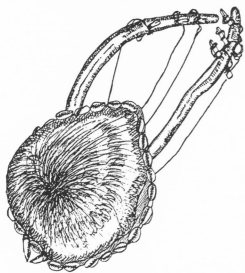

Akamba lyre.

As he approached old age, a second party, *kukula kwa kali*, celebrated the promotion of the father to *atumia ma kivalo*, full elder. He was now an old man, allowed to carry a three-legged stool, *muumbo*, so that he could sit among men and help in serious decision making. He also carried a forked staff as a sign of responsibility and wore a traditional gown made from black-and-white colobus monkey skins. A full elder checked over the cattle, carried out burial ceremonies, marked weather changes, and ran *thome*, the talking place where law was administered, visitors shared their journeys, and stories were told.

Near the end of his life, a man became *atumia ma kisuka*, senior elder. Now he was very old and was given great respect for the wisdom of his years. Regarded as a holy man, he was consulted during difficult times and on important issues.

As Europeans settled Kenya, the Akamba realized they would have to adopt new lifestyles. Once primarily hunters and warriors, they became traders, exchanging their arrow poisons, iron, and ivory for beads, copper, cotton, and salt. Several major events forced further changes. The Uganda Railway opened up Kenya to more settlers, a disease called rinderpest destroyed the cattle herds, the elephants that provided ivory diminished, and several droughts left insufficient crops to feed the people.

Long-established traditions began to disappear. The Akamba became craftsmen and farmers, tending crops of coffee, maize, vegetables, and fruit. They learned how to carve wood, plait baskets woven from fibers of baobab and wild fig trees, and create iron and copper jewelry and spears.

Like the chameleon in the Akamba story "Peace and Quiet" (page 49), these people have learned to adapt to their changing environment and find new ways to prosper and improve.

Kanga.

Who Are the Akamba?

From My Journal

July 14, 1988

Cottar's Camp, Maasai Mara National Reserve

It was an excellent day. A long game drive, an evening around the campfire, and stories told by Jackson, an Akamba *mzee*.

On the game drive we saw the carcass of a leopard's kill, a wildebeest tucked in the crook of a tree. We knew the leopard would remain nearby, so we quietly searched, and it was Kagathi's eagle eyes that finally found the cat, camouflaged as he slept under a bush. Only the slight movement of his breathing gave him away as his spots gently heaved up and down.

We also saw a magnificent black-maned lion who was being relentlessly pestered by flies. He finally retreated into the bushes, and we could hear the grunts and rustlings of his pride as they welcomed him. We could smell a rotting carcass.

This is the time of the migration, and there are thousands of wildebeest. Kagathi said, "Every day is Christmas for the lions, food everywhere." We ate our picnic lunch beneath an acacia tree, surrounded by these awkward animals described as being "made by a committee."[13]

Ph.13. Wildebeest.

They look like a medley of leftovers, and they are constantly grunting back and forth, "I'm here. Are you here? I'm hungry. Are you hungry? I'm ugly. Are you ugly? Unh! Unh! Henh! Henh! Aanh! Aanh!" They answer some unidentifiable signal and suddenly fall in line, simply following the one before, over ravines and across the savannah.

We spent over an hour following an elusive cheetah who was on the prowl for gazelle.[14] She charged three times but missed each chance. The rest of the time, she rippled through the long grass, only her ears revealing her location. Occasionally she would stop on a termite mound and lift her head, sniffing into the wind that tossed the wheat tassels around her. Eventually she disappeared, and the gazelle gave thanks for another day.

Ph.14. An elusive cheetah.

We saw zebra, topi, hartebeest, impala, and giraffe. We heard constant birdsong. And we were surrounded by wind and grass and endless skies.[15]

Ph.15. Wind, grass, and endless skies.

Ph.16. Jackson, an excellent teller.

After dinner, the finale: stories told as the crickets sang and the bats darted through the night. Occasionally a lion grunted and a hyena laughed in the darkness as Jackson[16] told tales of chameleon, rabbit, and a giant. He was an excellent teller, following the tradition of his grandparents. He said he could tell stories "until morning." It was a perfect ending to our time here in the Maasai Mara.

I wonder if the cheetah feeds tonight.

Peace and Quiet
Retold by Heather McNeil

Early one morning Tai the Vulture sailed across the skies, wings and beak open wide. "Lord of the Skies!" he screeched.[17] "Master of the Wind! I eat the flesh of lions and sail on the wings of death!"

On the earth below, hidden in an acacia tree, Kinyonga the Chameleon opened one eye. "Vulture is at it again," he moaned. "Bragging, always bragging." He closed his eye and was immediately *toweka*, invisible, in the greenness of the acacia leaves.

Ph.17. Lord of the Skies.

Tai screamed again. "Master of the Wind! Champion of the Hunt! I drink the blood of elephants and sail on the wings of death!"

"Oh, do be quiet, Tai!" thought Kinyonga. He opened the other eye. "Your screaming makes my head hurt." His eye shut and—*toweka!*—all that could be seen was *rangi ya mti*, the greenness of the tree.

"Lord of the Wind! Master of the Skies! I bring death to all!"

"All you bring is noise!" muttered the lizard. Both eyes snapped open and rotated toward the sky. "Lord of the Wind, indeed!" Kinyonga crawled headfirst down the trunk of the tree and onto the hard, dry, red earth. He rested quietly, his skin gradually changing color until, once again—*toweka!*—but this time into *rangi ya mwekundu*, the redness of the earth. He waited, camouflaged from view, until the huge bird circled overhead.

"Lord of the Skies! Master of Death! I—"

"Enough!" shouted Kinyonga. "All you are, Tai, is Lord of the Garbage Dump! Ha!"

Tai looked but saw nothing. He circled closer, his head rotating and his eyes searching to find the speaker of those irritating words. He could see only earth and grass and acacia trees. But there was that bodiless voice again.

"Tai, you are indeed Master. Master Junkman, Scavenger of Leftovers!" Kinyonga was so pleased with his cleverness that he forgot to keep his eyes closed. He looked up to find Vulture, and Vulture finally saw Chameleon. He dove toward the earth, talons outstretched and beak clacking. The tiny lizard scuttled back up the tree, fading into the leaves—*toweka!* But Vulture was approaching quickly, too quickly to stop his approach. BLAM! The huge bird crashed into a branch and found his beak and claws full of *hapana kitu*, nothing. Vulture toppled to the ground.

"Ha!" laughed Kinyonga. "Where's your bragging voice now, Tai?"

Tai hissed. "Where's your tasty body, Kinyonga? One gulp and you're gone."

Kinyonga laughed again. "I think I shall call you Mtawala wa Hewa, Lord of the Air, because that is all you can catch—air. Ha!"

Vulture screamed with fury. "You think you are so clever, lizard? Then stop hiding and show yourself."

Kinyonga knew all he had to do was give up his camouflage and he would be a tasty tidbit for Tai. He remained hidden in the leaves. "I have an idea, Tai. You think you are so grand, so brave, so clever. Are you grand enough and brave enough and clever enough to win *shindano*, a race?"

"A race? I can win any race. I am Lord of the Skies, Master of the—"

"Yes, I've already heard that. Several times. Too many times. But now you can prove it. The race will be from here to the large rock on the banks of the Wuaso Ng'iro River."

Tai pranced back and forth, flapping his wings with eagerness. "And who is the unfortunate animal that shall race against me and lose?"

There was a long silence. Then, from out of the branches, came the bodiless voice of Kinyonga. "*Mimi*. It is I, Vulture. I shall race you and I shall win."

"You, Kinyonga? You?" Vulture's bald head and neck wobbled with laughter. "The lazy lizard wants to race against Tai, Master of the Wind. Oh, do be serious!"

"I am serious, you silly bird. Deadly serious!"

"And that is what you shall be, Kinyonga. *Kufa.* Dead."

"So, if I lose, I die."

"My belly rumbles with delight."

"And if you lose—"

"Impossible, lazy one."

"IF YOU LOSE, then I get what I want."

"Which is?"

"*Raha na kimya.* Peace and quiet. No more screeching or bragging from you. Agreed?"

"Agreed. Now come down out of that tree, and we shall begin."

"If I come down out of this tree, Tai, then I shall end. In your beak. No, you go ahead and start the race. I will meet you at the river."

Vulture laughed and laughed, confident that the slow and lazy chameleon could never crawl faster than he could fly. He hopped and fluttered, chuckling to himself and smacking his beak as he thought of the tasty morsel of lizard flesh he would soon be enjoying.

Now, all the time he was dancing about, he did not realize that Kinyonga was carefully, cautiously, quietly crawling down the acacia trunk. When he reached the ground, he waited until he was *rangi ya mwekundu*, the color of the red earth. Then he scampered behind Vulture, who was just preparing himself for flight, unaware of the tiny, invisible lizard. As the bird leaped off the ground, Kinyonga grabbed Vulture's tail feathers and hung on tightly. Tai sailed up into the sky, never suspecting that Chameleon was attached.

Tai flew toward the river, gracefully gliding on currents of wind. He took his time, occasionally glancing toward the earth but seeing no sign of Chameleon. "This is too easy," he thought. "Kinyonga hasn't a chance against me. I am Master of the Skies! Lord of the Universe! I am death on wings!"

Peace and Quiet

Finally, Tai saw the banks of the Wuaso Ng'iro River.[18] He began to circle, floating in closer and closer. He saw the rock Kinyonga had described and glided toward it. He circled once. No lizard. He circled again. Still no lizard. He flapped his wings, slowly dropped, extended his talons, and landed on the rock. Tai screeched in triumph.

And then he heard a tiny voice from beneath him on the rock. "Watch where you are landing, Tai. Did you not see me waiting for you?"

Kinyonga now lives a life of *raha na kimya*, peace and quiet, in the acacia tree. Tai flies nowhere nearby. And that makes Kinyonga *furaha sana*, very happy.

Ph.18. The Wuaso Ng'iro River.

Stories from the Akamba

Original Translation

A long time ago Vulture met with Chameleon. They started to chase one another. So they were going to race for ten miles to see who would be first.

The vulture told the chameleon, "You go ahead. Me, I'll be behind because I'll pass in the air."

The chameleon told him "OK, you start. Then I'll start. And we'll meet there."

The chameleon was so smart. Just as the vulture was about to take off, he managed to grab the tail. Then the vulture took off. When he got to the place where they were going, the vulture landed, and the chameleon said, "Watch out. You are sitting on me."

The vulture cried out, "Oops! When did you arrive?"

The chameleon got the prize.

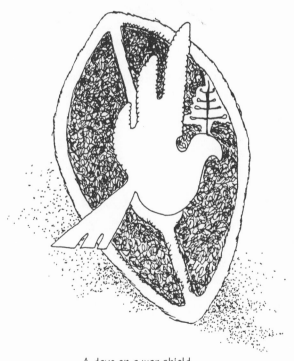

A dove on a war shield.

Tips on the Telling

Tips

- Before telling this story, become familiar with chameleons. Visit a pet store and watch one. Or visit your library and read about them; I recommend *Chameleons: Dragons in the Trees* by James Martin (1991). The photographs by Art Wolfe are amazing and will give you an appreciation of how finely adapted these creatures are to their life on the savannah.

- To tell a story well, you must know all the characters. Read about vultures, too, and about acacia trees and camouflage.

- Stories are best when they are not memorized. This story has a great deal of conversation, which should be used only as a beginning point for the individual teller. Add your own original ideas and words.

- The characters in this story are complete opposites. Try using distinctive voices and body movements to convey this difference: unhurried speech and slow head turns for the chameleon, loud voice and quick jerks and struts for the vulture. As always, keep the special voices and movements controlled.

- This story lends itself to tandem telling with a partner. Assign the two parts and establish your character. If you don't know immediately who should be assigned which role, try reading through the story both ways; usually, once you hear it, you'll know which part fits best. It's fun to work with another person's energy, but it does mean more memorization, because you each need to know your cues.

Stories from the Akamba

Stories from the Kipsigis

Who Are the Kipsigis?

At least 2,000 years ago, a convergence of cultures from Sudan, Ethiopia, and the Rift Valley of Kenya resulted in tribes described by scholars as the Southern Nilotic Group. The group has two branches, the Omotic and the Kalenjin. The latter is broken down into northern and southern divisions. The Kipsigis are part of the southern division, and they occupy an area from Lake Victoria in the west to lakes Nakuru and Naivasha in the east. The main city is Kericho, which is also the name given to the district.

Much in traditional Kipsigis society was determined by the sacred number, four. There were four regions, or *emotinwek*, governed by a four-pronged leadership: *kiruogindet neo*, the great judge; *poysiek ab puriosiek*, the oldest group of warriors; four *kiptainek ab puriosiek*, chiefs of the warriors; and *kiptaya neo nebo murenek*, the great chief of the warriors. In more recent times this system has been restructured and now comprises a great judge, *kokwotinwek*, who rules over several villages (*nganaset*), plus a judgment council, *kok*, that reconciles clan disputes.

Simi—a double-edged dagger.

The Kipsigis no longer follow the nomadic-pastoral lifestyle of long ago, punctuated by dramatic cattle raids against the Maasai, Kisii, and Luo. Over centuries, Kipsigis culture spontaneously underwent changes that prepared it for modern economic society, adjusting to inadequate rainfall, pastureland, and manpower by withdrawing to the highlands and learning to grow crops. Today the Kipsigis specialize in raising domestic animals and cultivating tea, pyrethrum, and corn. Finger millet is also a cash crop and is tended only by men, a custom unique to the Kipsigis.

The traditional Kipsigis lived in circular huts that were built by the entire community, not individual families—another tradition practiced only by the Kipsigis. Each hut had a cone-shaped roof covered with grass and supported by a central pole. The hut was large enough to be divided into two sections by a mud wall. One area was for the sheep and goats, for the rituals of marriage, and for the receiving of male guests. The other section contained the kitchen and the living quarters for the mother and children.

The reception area of every home featured a hole in the ground containing the all-important beer gourd. A pamphlet about the Kipsigis, distributed by the Text Book Centre of Nairobi, states, "To receive a guest into the house without offering him beer is the greatest lack of respect one can imagine."

When men gathered, the guests sat on the ground or on benches in a circle around the gourd and sipped the beer through long vegetable tubes.

Community and tradition have played an important role in Kipsigis culture. Adult initiation ceremonies highlighted this importance dramatically, for children were not considered to be Kipsigis until after the rites had been performed. In fact, the word *Kipsigis* may mean "people of the birth," referring to the ritual of circumcision, a figurative birth into adulthood.

Initiation was a lengthy process. A girl's initiation once took as long as two years; a boy's, up to three. Today, if practiced at all, the ritual lasts only several months. During the process, six childhood ceremonies were performed, including the extraction of the lower incisor teeth and the piercing of ears. The celebration began with the entire *kokwet* (a parish of approximately 100 homes) participating in dancing and solemn beer drinking. The male and female candidates were dressed in special skins and adorned with pendants and shells. The boys wore hoods of feathers, and multicolored masks with eye holes. Ornamentation for girls was even more fanciful, made from cheap market goods or broken pots. The dressing ceremony took many hours and was followed by a time for play and laughter.

The real ritual then began. The elaborate costumes were replaced with untreated goatskins, and the candidates' heads were shaved. Circumcision was performed on the boys, clitoridectomy on the girls, after which the initiates were segregated by gender and taken to special huts.

The girls remained isolated as long as twenty months, covering themselves with animal-skin hoods to prevent recognition when they had to go outside. They spent their time tanning animal hides and making clothes, including a bridal dress of animal skin softened with the oil of castor seeds and decorated with pearls and shells. They were not allowed to use chairs or beds, but sat and slept on platforms of dried mud. During the seventh month, instruction in the secrets of the Kipsigis people began.

At the end of the isolation period came *ngetundet*, "the coming out." Girls who were once slender adolescents emerged as considerably heavier young women. Both genders put away their hoods but were required to wear *nariet*, a veil of pearls, shells, or chains, hanging down from the forehead and covering the eyes. They were now Kipsigis and could officially enter the tribe upon marriage.

The Kipsigis believed in one god, Cheptalil, who was the creator and the master of heaven and earth. He was considered always good; the existence of evil in the world was attributed to mysterious spirits, or to spells cast by witch doctors. If a witch doctor was proven to be a wizard—one who had caused evil—he would be strangled. But witch doctors could also be herbalists, who were healers and doctors.

These ancient traditions of the Kipsigis are not as prevalent today. Ceremonies are abbreviated, portions of families are scattered to the cities, and children are learning new ways in schools. But the people remain strong in their agricultural abilities and knowledge of animal husbandry.

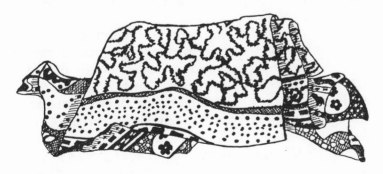

Kanga.

From My Journal

February 21, 1987

Kericho

Yesterday, on the way to Kericho, we stopped to watch tea pickers. The tea grows for miles, covering the rolling hills with lush green. The pickers wear heavy plastic vests to protect themselves as they push through the dense bushes. They carry long bamboolike poles that are laid across the tops of the bushes, and they pick whatever grows above the stick. They throw the leaves in a basket on their backs, which hold about three to four kilos. The tea is weighed,[19] and the picker is paid the equivalent of $.65 per kilo.

Ph.19. Weighing tea.

We also saw women picking pyrethrum, a daisylike flower used to make insecticide. Kagathi joined in the picking, which made the women laugh with delight, but when I tried to help, they objected loudly.

In Kericho, a quiet, nontourist town, we visited a tin factory, where the men make trunks, pans, buckets, and candle holders. We walked through the market; I particularly remember watching a man purchase about a dozen squawking, flapping chickens, then walk away with them dangling from his hands, upside down and completely docile.

That night we sat on the lawn of the cottage, and I told Kagathi about Crazy Horse as grey clouds gathered and thunder rumbled.

Today, just outside of Kericho, Kagathi stopped to chat with several young men selling newspapers. They laughed and punched each other, looking like macho men everywhere. One Kipsigis man named Samwel offered to take us to his home for stories. Outside, several men were pounding bags of corn to remove the kernels, and children appeared from nowhere. At first, no one seemed able to tell us any stories. Samwel said, "When we were young, we told stories in the evening. But now they are forgotten." Finally, his sister came out and told a haunting story about a monkey who wants to marry a woman and then eat her.[20] Samwel insisted on translating, so we just sat in the van under a tree and listened. I took the usual family portrait, and Samwel promised to send me more stories.

Ph.20. Samwel's sister, on the left, told the story of "Monkey's Feast."

Tonight, I am watching the sun set over Lake Victoria.[21] The air is heavy and full of the promise of rain. Below the room, I hear the voices of Kenyan children playing on a swing, several turbanned Indian men in serious conversation, an American family at the pool, and a British murmur coming from the patio. Huge black birds are circling, there's rain falling on the other side of the lake, and the sky is filled with grey and pink clouds.

Ph.21. Sunset over Lake Victoria.

Later: The storm arrived. Strong winds blew rain under the door, soaking the rug. I tried to open the door to go down for dinner and had to brace myself against the wall to keep from being blown across the room. A soggy bat was swept onto the porch and has collapsed, trembling, in a corner.

Stories from the Kipsigis

Monkey's Feast
Retold by Heather McNeil

A long time ago there was a woman so beautiful, so beautiful that she loved her own beauty more than anything or anyone. She refused to marry, believing that no man was her equal, and she spent her days gazing at her own reflection in the water pools.

One day a man entered the village. He was a stranger, but so handsome, so handsome. He wore robes of monkey skins, and he walked straight and tall and proud. The young man stopped at the home of the beautiful woman and presented her parents with a gift of two cows. The parents asked him, "What do you want here?," and he answered, "To speak with your oldest daughter." The next day he returned with two more cows, and the next day, two more. Every day,

after giving away his cows, he would walk to the water pools, sit beside the beautiful woman, and ask her to be his wife.

Now, this woman had a younger sister. She was not as beautiful as the older girl, but she was clever and strong. Every day, while the man was courting her sister at the water pools, the young girl hid in the bushes, watching, listening, wondering.

She heard her sister refuse the man many times. She saw him roll his eyes and clamp his teeth with disappointment. And she saw how her sister was always looking at her own reflection, not at him, so that she did not see his hands clenched in fists of anger.

Every day the man came with gifts of cows for the parents, and with words like honey, sweet with promise, for the oldest daughter. At last, the woman agreed to marry this man, so handsome, so handsome, whom she believed to be her equal.

Hiding in the bushes, the younger girl heard her sister say, "Yes." She saw the man chatter his teeth with delight and dig his fingers, like claws, into the earth. The older girl saw nothing but her own face in the pool of water.

The next day the man appeared again with cows for the woman's parents. This time when they asked, "What do you want here?" he answered, "I want to marry your oldest daughter."

They asked their daughter, "Do you agree that this man is to marry you?" She agreed.

"We shall have tea in celebration," said the mother, and she invited the man into their home. The man agreed. And because the mother's face was turned toward the fire and the father was thinking about his new cows and the girl was looking at her reflection in the teacup, no one saw what the man did.

Except for the younger sister. She stood outside, looking, looking, looking through the window. She saw him swallow the tea, and the cup, and the plate. She saw him roll his eyes and chatter his teeth and beat his chest with his fists.

"This is not a man," thought the girl. "This is a monkey pretending to be a man!"

The girl ran inside. "Sister, I must speak with you!" She grabbed her sister's hand and pulled her outside. But when she told her what she had seen, the older girl just laughed. "You are a jealous fool! He is not a monkey. He is a man, so handsome, so handsome. And I shall marry him."

The woman returned to the celebration and sat beside the man who was to be her husband. And because the mother was busy cooking beans and the father was sleeping and the girl was dreaming of her wedding dress, no one saw what the man did.

Except for the younger sister. She stood outside, looking, looking, looking through the window. She saw the man catch flies in the air and lizards on the ground. She saw him drop them in his mouth, swallow, and lick his lips.

The girl ran back inside the house. "Sister, I must speak with you!" She pulled her sister outside and told her what she had seen." The man you are going to marry is not a man. I tell you, he is a monkey!"

Stories from the Kipsigis

But her sister would not listen. "You do not want me to marry that man because you are jealous."

"I do not want you to marry that man because he is a monster!"

"He is not a monster. He is not a monkey. He is a man, and I will marry him!"

And the very next day, she did. The younger sister watched as the beautiful woman and her handsome new husband walked down the road to his home.

She followed them.

That night, when all the forest was asleep, the girl was watching, watching, watching from above in the branches of a tree. She saw a monkey come out of the house and run into the forest.[22] She heard the monkey call out to all the animals, "Tomorrow there will be a feast. Elephant! Lion! Buffalo! I promise you a delicious feast!" Then she saw the monkey run back inside the house.

The girl knew that the feast would be her sister.

The next morning the girl came to the house and asked the man if she could help her older sister. "Of course," he said, his eyes burning like white fire. "You can gather wood for all the food we will be cooking today. We are having a feast."

The girl handed him a pot she had brought with her. "Then I will need water for all that cooking. Bring me water from the stream."

The man took the pot, never noticing the tiny crack along the bottom. He walked to the stream, dipped the pot in, and filled it with water. But by the time he stood up and turned to walk back home, the pot was empty. Again he dipped the pot, and again it emptied itself. Over and over this foolish man tried to fill the pot.

Ph.22. A monkey ran into the forest.

While he was doing this, the young girl was searching for her older sister. She found her tied with vines, her beautiful eyes large and liquid with fear. The girl untied her, and they ran back to the home of their parents.

When the man finally returned to his home, he found that his wife and her sister were gone, and there was no fire or water cooking. When Lion, Elephant, and Buffalo arrived, hungry for the promised feast, they found only Monkey.

So they ate him.

Original Translation

A long time ago there was a monkey. There was a lady. This lady was so beautiful, she was confused as to who was to marry her.

A monkey came. This monkey was very mischievous. He tried all his best until he was able to convince this girl. He came to the girl's home, he stayed with the parents. He was asked, "What do you want here?"

"I want to marry this girl."

The girl was also asked, "Do you agree that this monkey is to marry you?"

The monkey was pretending to be a man, standing on two legs. This monkey was given tea. He sat down and drank the tea. The younger sister of the girl was peeking through the window. She saw the monkey swallowing everything with the cup. She ran and told her sister, "This person is swallowing everything."

"It is not true that he is swallowing everything."

The girl looked through the window again, and she saw the monkey swallowing flies. She ran and told the people, "He is swallowing flies. I told you once he was swallowing the cup and the kettle, and you never agreed."

The sister came that never saw anything.

The monkey asked the parents to be allowed to marry this girl. Now the monkey was given this woman, but he was not to take her at this time. He was to wait until tomorrow.

He waited until tomorrow. Then he came and took her from the home. He took her to his home. He had a plan to swallow this woman. He went and called all the animals—lion, elephant—to tell them, "Tomorrow we are having a big feast."

Then the monkey arranged for the sister to come and help him in the household.

The sister was very keen. The monkey had a plan to swallow her, but the younger sister knew they were to be swallowed.

The monkey boiled water in a big pot. The sister was checking, "What is this man doing here?" Then the animals came, and they found the monkey had not finished his arrangements.

Now the monkey was given a broken pot. He went to the river to bring water.

Meanwhile the lady was planning to run away because she thought, "I do not want to be boiled. I do not want to be eaten by this monkey."

The monkey was still getting water from the river. When he returned, there was no one at home. Then the guests came, preparing to feast. They wanted to feast *now*. So the monkey was eaten by the animals.

Monkey's Feast

Notes and Tips on the Telling

Notes

- I knew that somewhere, hidden inside the confusing translation of this story, was a tale worth telling. Samwel's English was not as fluent as Kagathi's, which probably accounts for the contradictions and omissions in the original telling. I should have asked more questions of Samwel in order to clarify the misunderstandings. Instead, I had to use a combination of common sense, imagination, and knowledge of African stories to create my version.

- As I began rewriting the story, I had trouble believing that the woman would not be able to tell that her fiancé was a monkey. But then I remembered other such stories: "The Girl Who Married a Ghost," from the Nisqualli people of North America (published in *The Girl Who Married a Ghost and Other Tales from the North American Indian*, collected by Edward S. Curtis and edited by John Bierhorst [1978]), and "Sedna," from the Eskimo people (*The Song of Sedna* by Robert D. SanSouci [1981]; *Sedna* by Beverly Brodsky McDermott [1975]; and *Spirits, Heroes & Hunters from North American Indian Mythology* by Marion Wood [1981]). Both tell of a beautiful woman who is blinded by her love for a man from the spiritual world. After all, don't we often see only what we want to see?

- I was also surprised by the fact that the younger sister is so strong and outspoken. She even convinces a *man* to fetch water! That is not common in Kenyan cultures. But then I considered the fact that the story was told to me by a young woman. And it is, after all, a story, intended to teach and entertain, not necessarily relate facts.

Tips

- This story is appropriate only for certain audiences. There are underlying elements of abuse and cannibalism that need to be considered. Use this one with older listeners who are interested in tradition and culture and who won't get affixed to the implausible notion of a woman marrying a monkey.

- Straight and simple. That's how the story should be told. No dramatics, no odd voices, no interruptions in rhythm (which is why this is the only story in this collection without Swahili). The foreboding of danger should become evident through a few appropriate pauses or facial expressions.

- Say the last line clearly; don't let any word be lost. Your audience will be stunned. But if your voice trails off, your audience will only be confused.

Stories from the Taita

Who Are the Taita?

They call themselves the People of the Hills. In their mysterious tradition, disaster is attributed to the anger of dead ancestors and evil spirits embodied in snakes. Rituals, powerful medicines, and the curses of sorcerers are part of an intricate religion developed by this society, which is dedicated to peace and harmony among its people.

The Taita may have come from the Kiliminjaro region, migrating north to Dabida, Sagalla, and Kasigau, the three Taita hills. Originally they were hunters, but when Tsavo Park was established as a game reserve, the hunting became restricted to the hills and the game soon left, so today the Taita are farmers and craftsmen. They excel in basketry, pottery, and the working of leather, iron, and wood. To compensate for the desert climate, the Taita have developed an impressive irrigation system for their cash crops, vegetables and tobacco: water is channelled by furrows and by hollow banana-stem pipes that extend for more than two miles. Family gardens, tended by the women, yield millet, maize, sugarcane, bananas, beans, and cassava.

The Taita of long ago, when the stories originated, created a social structure based on the principle of *dasikirana*, "We understand one another." Each community was a neighborhood with its own name, and marriages remained within the neighborhood. Everyone knew the expected customs, *mizengo*, a state of affairs that was thought to promote friendliness.

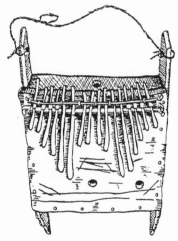

Mbira—thumb piano.

The homes, *nyumba*, consisted of mud walls over post-and-wattle frames, topped by a thatched or corrugated iron roof. Outbuildings included granaries and a shelter for livestock. The homestead was surrounded by a smooth, swept courtyard, often ringed by boulders or a hedge with a gate.

Before the age of three, children were not considered responsible, because they could not judge right or wrong. After approximately three years, they reached the age of *akili*, sense, determined by their ability to perform certain actions. At this point they were aware of their rights and could hold anger in their hearts.

Female infants underwent clitoridectomy; boys were circumcised between the ages of eight and twelve. At puberty, initiation rites transformed a girl into *mwai*, a maiden, and a boy into *mdaβana*, a youth or bachelor. An adolescent girl worked in the fields and helped cook and serve food. She also joined work clubs, receiving payment for her gardening skills. An adolescent boy was less integrated into the work of men. As *mwana*, a child, he was allowed to attend ritual ceremonies, but as *mdaβana*, he was excluded. He was expected to help his father with daily chores, and some boys joined girls in forming work clubs.

When a bachelor began courtship, his main concern was acquiring bridewealth. To accumulate enough, he often relied on his father's assistance. The bride was sometimes kidnapped in a mock abduction or encouraged to elope. Once married, the newlyweds lived in the home of the husband's parents until their first child was born; then they could move into their own home, built by both sets of parents.

Marriage was undertaken not as a response to passion or love, but to benefit both families involved. The wife's role was to bear children and tend the home and garden. The husband was required to provide the house and fields, to tend the herds, and to perform heavy labor. Children were parental assets, "the greatest good." Sons guaranteed the father's progress through the social ranks, and when a son had a son, the child's father would claim he had "begotten his father," *wava ndee*, naming the child after the infant's paternal grandfather. The grandfather's status was now enhanced.

Taita tradition featured a fixed social hierarchy. Males ranked higher than females; initiated youths and maidens ranked higher than noninitiates. The married were superior to the unmarried, and those with children were superior to the childless. Independent householders were more important than those still under a father's supervision. The highest echelon comprised the old men with sons and grandsons, large herds, and fields to lend to younger men. They had influence, wealth, ritual knowledge, and possession of personal shrines. A pool of neighborhood elders acted as a governmental body, listening to disputes and making decisions enforced by the power of curses, oaths, and ordeals.

Perhaps one of the most fascinating aspects of Taita culture was their religion, for it attempted to alleviate all disharmony through a combination of soul-searching, sacrifice, ritual, and divination. It was not a religion based on worship and performance, but on responding to the mystic agents they believed were involved in their daily lives. Grace Gredys Harris's book *Casting Out Anger: Religion Among the Taita* (1978) is a detailed account of that religion, portions of which will be described here for a better understanding of the history of these people and their stories.

The Taita believed that sickness, death, misfortunes, plague, and drought were caused by mystic agents who had been angered by the actions of a person or community. Peace, *sere*, was the greatest desire of Taita life. Committed to nonviolence and desirous of good fortune, the Taita undertook the ritual of *kutasa* to determine the moral cause of any unhappiness and to appease the agents. Through *kutasa*, all hidden angers and buried resentments that might be associated with the unhappiness were released. The ritual was performed in a squatting position, with the arms across the knees, one hand holding a container of sugarcane beer, fermented cane juice, or water. The performer called out to the offended spiritual agents while spraying out mouthfuls of liquid. His or her heart, *ngolo*, had to be "cool" and all requests for blessings and a release from anger, sincere. Sometimes the ritual was accompanied by *kizongona*, an animal offering, or *kuroya*, a gift.

The Taita believed that Mlungu, Creator of the Universe, could send drought or plague if angered by the moral rottenness of a community. Ancestral shades, the spirits of dead ancestors, could cause misfortune if they were offended. The dangerous mystical anger of living humans and animals could be aroused by ignoring their rights or by inconsiderate behavior. For instance, the death of an infant was seen as an attack on the parents for irresponsibility. An offended wife could harm her husband, his herd, or their children through her anger. A maternal uncle, considered a third parent, could cause misfortune to befall his sister's children if anger remained unresolved between the siblings. The offended one's heart became "hot," *modo*, and *kuzigona ngolonyi*, looking within the heart, would be required to uncover the forgotten reason for anger.

The spiritual rituals of the Taita always involved eliminating immorality, evil, or unhappiness. It was not the anger but the denial of it and the resulting resentment that was considered dangerous.

Traditions other than *kutasa* that were observed to bring about *sere* included:

- The practice of *Figi*, holy medicine used by *Mfigiki*, the Defender (a position held by a tribesman), to assure the safety of the neighborhood. The combined performances of sprinkling *kioro*, medicine; feasting on a sacrificial goat; and *kutasa* from all the men protected the innocent community members by endangering the wicked, such as sorcerers or enemies.

- Rainmaking. *Mnyeshi-vui*, the rainmaker (another tribal position), supervised a ceremony that would assure the arrival of the all-important rains. *Kioro* of twigs gathered from special bushes on the peak of Yale (a nearby mountain), combined with water, was used, plus divination of a sacrificial goat's entrails, and *kutasa*. If the determination was that the rains would come, there would be *mbeka*, an all-night dance of married men and women.

- Worship at holy shrines containing medicines used to alleviate illness or to bring prosperity. Care of the communal shrines was assigned through lineage; individually owned shrines were acquired at different stages in the social hierarchy and represented the achievement of wealth and wisdom. The shrines included *Mfuko*, Bag; *Kifumbi*, Stool; *Mmanga*, Bell; and *Lufu*, Knife. Each was anointed through a ceremony

Who Are the Taita?

of a special offering and required careful attention, or misfortune would occur.

In opposition to these efforts to ensure peace and harmony was sorcery, the practice of using spells and medicines to intentionally harm others. *Mlogi*, a sorcerer, motivated by greed and envy, used *magemi*, curses, to cause illness, poverty, or death. He could alter the fertility of humans and crops with herbal preparations hidden in food, homes, or fields. Sorcery could also be produced by anyone performing *kutasa* insincerely. If someone was proven to be a sorcerer, the Executioners' Society, comprising a select group of elders, would administer *mbaro*, medicine, with an unconditional and irreversible curse to eliminate the evil. They would force the guilty person to swallow *mugule*, the ordeal medicine that would kill the sorcerer. Otherwise, Mlungu would bring drought or plague to any community in which there was uncontrolled sorcery or immorality.

Death was perceived as a crossing from the world of the living to the world of the dead. Observances for the dead lasted as long as a week and included the chief mourners' shaving their heads. A month after death, the funeral was performed, at which point mourning ended, symbolized by the mourners' cutting their hair that had grown since the death. Several elders spoke remembrances, and the deceased was buried.

Many years later, at a time determined through divination or by a "message" of misfortune, the deceased's skull would be exhumed by the eldest son. It was cleaned, wrapped in banana leaves, smeared with the stomach contents of a sacrificial sheep, and placed in *Ngomenyi*, a designated area usually surrounded by a grove of trees. The most recently deceased were placed in the front row. Women's skulls were placed to the left of the husband; barren women were not allowed in *Ngomenyi*. The skulls of convicted thieves and sorcerers were also denied placement unless the person had requested *kutasa* and appropriate divination before he or she died.

Perhaps these traditions of ritual and sacrifice seem frightening in today's world. However, their practice was designed by a society who realized the importance of a healthy life, whether it was animal or human. Each time *kutasa* was performed or a diviner tried to determine the moral cause of an illness, the People of the Hills hoped to solve a mystery and come closer to achieving *sere*, peace.

From My Journal

March 1, 1987

Mombasa

Mombasa. Noisy, crowded, dirty. The people are interesting to watch because there is so much variety. Exotic Moslem women draped in black *bui-bui*, with downcast eyes and secret faces. Samburu warriors, red *shukas*, robes, tossed over one shoulder, spears in hand, and looking positively out-of-place as they wait for a bus. Businessmen in business suits; women wrapped in the traditional red-and-yellow cloths called *kangas*; children in hand-me-down shorts and polyester dresses; tourists in everything. We had a cold drink at a Turkish cafe, and I heard a cornucopia of languages around me—Italian, German, English, Swahili, French. Like all large cities Mombasa is alive and scurrying with action and noise. But I miss the call of the ring-necked dove that woke me on safari and the grunts of the lions that echoed in the night.

The day began with a perfectly gorgeous game drive in Tsavo that gave me a chance to say good-bye to the birds and animals of Kenya for a return to the United States in four days. (I *will* be back!) I saw one new animal, the eland, largest of the antelopes, always on the move and very elusive. There were elephants, their backs sprayed red from dust baths. I saw impala, giraffe, gazelle, waterbuck, and a magnificent crested eagle. We were the only ones around because Tsavo is so large. It was cool, dustless, and quiet.

Kagathi had arranged for us to visit a Taita family, so we drove into Mwatate and picked up Danson, a young man about sixteen years old who directed us to his home high up in the misty hills.[23] The women were lovely, the men small and solid, and at least eighteen people gathered with us in the front room of a cement-block house.[24] At first they didn't understand what we wanted, so Kagathi told a story about a man who is hired by the king to kill flies. He has a huge club that he uses to smash the insects, as well as anything that happens to be under the flies. The story ends with his smashing a fly that landed on the king's head, killing the king in the process, of course. The family laughed and laughed and then the storytelling began.

One particularly exciting moment for me was when Danson told about a time of drought when Rabbit steals water from the well that everyone else helped to dig. It was basically the same story that I have told for years, a forerunner to "Bre'r Rabbit and the Tar Baby." In Danson's version the rabbit is finally caught by a crab hiding in the water of the well. The rabbit begs not to be thrown into the air, the crab throws him anyway, he lands on his feet, and he runs away. In the version I have

Ph.23. Danson's home high up in the misty hills.

Ph.24. A large group gathered in front of a cement-block house. (Danson is wearing the Mickey Mouse tee-shirt.)

told, Rabbit is caught by getting stuck to a man made of tar, then begs the animals not to "burst" him by filling him with all his favorite foods and then throwing him into the forest. Which they do, of course, and he runs away free. It was incredible to hear the original story that had traveled over continents, oceans, and generations.

When we went back down the mountain, Danson told Kagathi to pull over at a certain spot so he could tell us a legend about the marsh below us. Very solemnly he spoke about a woman who married and gave birth to a snake. The snake and other evil spirits continue to live in that marsh.

Rabbit's Drum
Retold by Heather McNeil

A long time ago there was a farmer whose garden was being destroyed by an elephant. Day after day, week after week, Tembo the Elephant ate all the farmer's *maharagwe* (beans), *nyanya* (tomatoes), and *maboga* (pumpkins). The farmer had nothing to eat, his children had nothing to eat, and *bustani*, the garden, was empty. So the farmer called a meeting to find someone who could stop Tembo.[25]

All the animals came to the meeting, including Sungura the Rabbit, clever, crafty, and quick. The farmer said, "I will give *ng'ombe mmoja*, one cow, to anyone who can catch the elephant who is eating *bustani yangu*, my garden."

"Oooh!" said all the animals. "*Ng'ombe mmoja!* That is a good offer."

So Mbuni the Ostrich[26] said she would try. She ran here. She ran there. She ran and ran for a day and a night, trying to catch Tembo. Finally, Mbuni gave up.

The farmer said, "I will give *ng'ombe wawili*, two cows, to anyone who can catch the elephant who is eating *bustani yangu*."

Ph.25. Tembo the Elephant.

"Aaah!" said the animals. *"Ng'ombe wawili!* That is a good offer."

So Mbweha the Jackal and Simba the Lion said they would try. They trotted. They stalked. They yipped and they roared. But after two days and two nights Mbweha and Simba gave up.

The farmer said, "I will give *ng'ombe watatu*, three cows, to anyone who can catch the elephant who is eating *bustani yangu*."

"Oooh! Aaah!" said the animals. *"Ng'ombe watatu.* That is the best offer." But no one would try, not even for three cows.

Except Sungura the Rabbit, clever, crafty, and quick. "I will catch Tembo," said Sungura.

Ph.26. Mbuni the Ostrich.

The farmer laughed. "How are you going to catch him? You are *mdogo sana*, very small, and Tembo is *mkubwa sana*, very big."

"Being *mkubwa* is not as important as being *akili*, clever," said Sungura. "I will catch Tembo, and you will pay me *ng'ombe watatu. Ndiyo?* Yes?"

"Ndiyo," said the farmer. *"Ng'ombe watatu."*

So the rabbit hopped—BBA! BBA! BBA!—into the farmer's garden. He found *boga kubwa sana*, a large pumpkin. He cut a hole at the top and dug out all the seeds and pulp. Then Sungura grabbed a stick, climbed inside the pumpkin, and slept.

DHON! DHON! DHON! Sungura woke up. DHON! DHON! DHON! The earth trembled. DHON! DHON! DHON! Tembo walked right over to the pumpkin that had Rabbit hiding inside. WHOOF! WHIFF! Sungura heard Elephant's searching trunk as it sniffed at the delicious pumpkin. WHOOF! WHIFF! GULP! Tembo swallowed the pumpkin, and Sungura rolled and tumbled about in the pumpkin as the pumpkin rolled and tumbled into the elephant's stomach.

Sungura waited until all was quiet, then he picked up his stick and—BOOM! BOOM! BOOM! Tembo stopped eating. BOOM! BOOM!

BOOM! Tembo began to run. BOOM! BOOM! BOOM! Tembo screamed because somebody was beating *ngoma*, a drum, inside his stomach!

BOOM! BOOM! BOOM! On and on ran Tembo. BOOM! BOOM! BOOM! On and on beat Sungura. BOOM! BOOM! BOOM! Tembo ran, Sungura drummed, until, finally, Tembo could run no more. Tembo crashed to the earth, the farmer speared the elephant, and then he cut open the stomach. Out rolled *boga ngoma*, the pumpkin drum, and out jumped Sungura. And the rabbit hopped home—BBA! BBA! BBA!—clever, crafty, quick, and RICH!

Stories from the Taita

Original Translation

A long time ago there was this one farmer. He was being bothered very much by these elephants trying to eat his crops. So he called a meeting of everybody. The rabbit offered himself to go and guard this man's farm.

"What are you going to do?" asked the farmer. "You are so small and the elephants are so big. What kind of arrangement will you do to keep the elephants away?"

"I'm going to do my own thing and you'll see."

The farmer had many pumpkins. The rabbit made a hole in one of them and took all the stuffing out. Then he got inside.

The elephants came, and one of them ate the pumpkin with the rabbit inside. The rabbit started playing the drum. The elephant started running. He was so exhausted, but still there were drums in his stomach.

The people caught this one elephant with the drums, and they killed him. They took the pumpkin out. The rabbit came out and ran away.

Notes and Tips on the Telling

Notes

It can be difficult for some listeners to accept the cruelty of the elephant's death, so I preface my telling with a discussion about how life has changed for the Taita. As civilization approaches—and sometimes encroaches on—the boundaries of animal reserves, people are forced to make choices between what is right for the animals and what is good for the people themselves. Life in Kenya is often a matter of survival: human vs. drought, human vs. illness, human vs. animal. In this farmer's eyes, the elephant must die in order that his family can survive.

Tips

- If you enjoy inviting participation, try dividing the audience into groups for the different sounds—BBA! BBA! (Rabbit hopping), DHON! DHON! DHON! (Elephant walking), WHOOF! WHIFF! (Elephant sniffing). Everyone joins in for the sound of the drum. You need to arrange this before you begin the telling, and you must establish cues so participants know when to begin. A hand gesture, a head nod, or a phrase that makes it obvious ("While Sungura slept, Tembo *stomped* into the garden....") can be used.

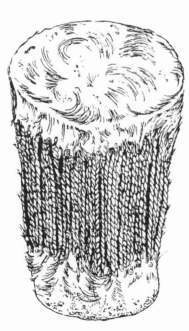

Ngoma—drum.

- This is a good story for creative dramatics. If you feel comfortable with movement, try to impersonate Ostrich, Lion, Elephant, and Rabbit. Or select children to act out the characters while you tell the story.

- The conclusion of the story, beginning with the first sound of the drum, needs to build in volume and speed. Establish your own pattern and sequence, but the audience should feel the annoyance and frustration of the elephant as he tries to escape from the drum but cannot.

- I made sure I brought back a small drum from Kenya to use with this story. Check your local import stores if you want to purchase one. Or, you can make a replica of a drum. Craft books such as *Make Your Own Musical Instruments* by Margaret McLean (1982) or *Making and Playing Musical Instruments* by Afken den Boer and Margot de Zeeuw (1989) are resources for ideas. A drum is not necessary, however; the voice is always available!

- A related classroom activity is "discovering" pumpkins and other gourds. Empty one out and beat on it (gently). Dry a gourd in the sun, or purchase a calabash at an import store so listeners can see how useful they are as storage containers or musical instruments. *The Complete Book of Nature Crafts* by Eric Carlson (1992) gives guidelines on making a gourd drum.

Rabbit's Drum

Water sweet, water fine,
Water, water will be mine!

Long ago there came a time of *ukosefu wa mvua*, no rain. The rivers were dry. The lakes were dry. The mud holes and the rock holes and the holes hidden inside old, soft logs, all were dry.

Without water, the animals had nothing to drink. And with nothing to drink, the animals knew they would soon die. So it was that Simba the Lion, Tumbili the Monkey, Mamba the Crocodile, Chui the Leopard, Kuro the Waterbuck, Ngiri the Warthog, and all the other animals came together, in peace, to talk about *maji*, water.

The lion began. "Who can find us water? Mamba, we must have water. Where is the water you swim in every day?"[27]

Ph.27. Simba wondered who would find water.

Crocodile wept dry tears. "There is no water. I do not swim anymore. I crawl on the earth, like Mjusi the lizard."

"Chui," said Simba, "we must have water. Where is the water you drink every day?"

Leopard choked and coughed. "There is no water. I do not drink anymore. I eat dust, like Muhanga the Aardvark in the termite hill."

"Kuro," said Simba, "we must have water. Where is the water that is always beside your feet?"[28]

Waterbuck pawed at the ground that was cracked with lines of death. "There is no water. There is only dust under my feet, as it is under all of our feet."

Lion asked each of the animals, and, to everyone's surprise, it was Ngiri the Warthog who had an answer.[29] "It is in the ground," said Ngiri.

"What did you say?" demanded Simba. "*Maji* is where?"

"In the ground."

"Where in the ground?"

Ph.28. Waterbuck stopping to drink.

"Deep. Sometimes, in my hole, I can smell it. But I cannot dig deep enough to find it."

"Then we must all dig," said Lion. "Everyone will dig, deep into the earth. And everyone will share in the water that we find."

All the animals agreed—except for Sungura, the lazy, lazy, rabbit. "You go ahead and dig. I will watch."

"If you do not dig," Lion growled, "then you do not drink." But Sungura just laughed.

Ph.29. Ngiri the Warthog knew how to find water.

So the animals began to dig. With paws and claws and tusks and teeth, they dug and they dug and they dug. It was chura kidogo, the smallest-of-frogs, who saw the first trickle of water come up out of the earth, and they began to sing:

Water sweet, water fine,
Water, water will be mine!
Be-deep! Be-deep! Be-deep!

Chura katikati, the middle-of-frogs, joined in as the water began to fill the hole:

Water sweet, water fine,
Water, water, will be mine!
Go-deep! Go-deep! Go-deep!

And, finally, chura kikubwa, the giant-of-frogs, sang:

Water sweet, water fine,
Water, water, will be mine!
Now-deep! Now-deep! Now-deep!

The animals began to drink. They sipped and slurped and lapped and licked—except for the lazy, lazy rabbit.

"You did not dig," said Simba, "so you will not drink." But the lazy, lazy rabbit just laughed.

In the morning, when the animals returned to the water hole, they found footprints in the mud, fresh footprints, and they all knew whose footprints they were. The lion called another meeting.

"The agreement was that all the animals would dig and all the animals would drink. But Sungura did not dig and Sungura WILL NOT DRINK!" Simba chose a monkey to guard the hole that night. All the other animals had a drink of cool, sweet water and then went back to their homes.

Ph.30. Tumbili waited.

Tumbili waited.[30] He looked up. He looked down. He looked behind him and all around. He wiggled and he squirmed, for he was a monkey. Finally, Tumbili decided to hide in the grass.

Just as the sun was ready to sleep for the night, down the road came that lazy, lazy rabbit. A gourd was swinging in one hand, a stick in the other, and Sungura was singing as he walked:

Water sweet, water fine,
Water, water will be mine!

He hit the water with his stick. PSSHH! Out popped Tumbili from the grass.

"Hello, Monkey. How are you this fine, fine evening?"

"Go away, Rabbit. You are not drinking any of this water."

"Why would I want any of that dirty water, Monkey, when I have all of this sweet, sweet water?"

"What sweet, sweet water?"

Rabbit dipped a finger into the gourd, licked it, and smacked his lips. "Mmmm, this water is as sweet as—honey!"

"As sweet as honey?"

"*Ndiyo*, Tumbili. Yes, Monkey. As sweet as *asali ya nyuki*."

"Where did you get that water, Rabbit? This hole has all the water there is."

"No, Monkey, that is not all the water." He dipped his finger again and licked it. "Mmmm."

"Let me taste your water, Sungura, so I can see if it is really as sweet as *asali ya nyuki*."

Rabbit poured the liquid—the sweet, thick, golden liquid, into Monkey's mouth. And Monkey drank every last drop.

"Tumbili, you drank all my water! Now what will I drink?"

"I am sorry, Sungura. Please, drink the water in the hole. Drink all you want."

And the rabbit, the lazy, lazy rabbit, did.

In the morning, Lion roared with anger. "Tumbili, why is more water gone?"

Monkey tried to explain, but all the animals just laughed. Lion chose another monkey to guard the water hole. The animals drank, then went home to their families.

Stories from the Taita

Monkey waited. He looked up. He looked down. He looked behind him and all around. He wiggled and he squirmed, for he was a monkey. Finally, Tumbili hid in the grass.

Just as the sun was ready to sleep for the night, down the road came that lazy, lazy rabbit, gourd swinging in one hand, a stick swinging in the other, as he walked and sang:

Water sweet, water fine,
Water, water will be mine!

Rabbit hit the water with his stick. PSSHH! Out popped Tumbili.

"Hello, Monkey. How are you this fine, fine evening?"

"Go away, Sungura. I know about you and how you tricked my brother."

"Oh, no. I did not trick your brother. I just gave him some of my sweet, sweet water."

"What sweet water, Rabbit? The only water is in this hole."

"No, Monkey. I have my own *maji*." Rabbit dipped a finger in the gourd, licked it, and smacked his lips. "Mmmm. Sweet as *asali ya nyuki*."

"As sweet as honey?"

"*Ndiyo*, Tumbili. Would you like to taste it?" Rabbit poured the liquid—the thick, sweet, golden liquid—into Monkey's mouth. And Monkey drank every last drop.

"Tumbili, you drank all my water! Now what will I drink?"

"I am so sorry, Sungura. Please, drink the water in the hole. Drink all you want."

And the rabbit, the lazy, lazy rabbit, did.

The next morning Lion roared and the animals laughed at Monkey.

Lion chose another monkey. And the next morning, another monkey. And the next morning, another monkey, until all the monkeys had had a chance, and the animals were not laughing any longer.

Water, Water Will Be Mine

Simba roared, "There are no more monkeys! Who will catch Sungura?"

Nyamaza. Silence. Nobody wanted to be tricked by Rabbit. Nobody wanted to be laughed at by the animals and roared at by Lion.

Simba asked each of the animals, one by one. "Ngiri? Chui? Mamba? Kuro?" Finally he came to Kaa, the crab. "Kaa, *you* will catch Sungura!"

Everyone looked at Kaa. His eye stalks bobbed up and down and his claw clicked and clacked. "Me? But I am only a crab."

"Yes," said Lion, "you are a crab. And where do crabs live?"

"In sand ... on rocks ... in the water!"

"Yes, Kaa, in the water. And what does the claw of a crab do?"

"Pinch ... scratch ... catch!"

"Yes, Kaa, they catch. Will you help us?"

Everyone looked at Kaa, and Kaa looked at everyone. "I will try."

Kaa scuttled down into the hole and disappeared under the water. Then all the animals had a cool drink and went home to their families.

Just as the sun was ready to sleep, down the road came that lazy, lazy rabbit, gourd in one paw, stick in the other, and he sang as he walked:

> Water sweet, water fine,
> Water, water will be mine!

Rabbit hit the water with his stick. PSSHH!

Nothing happened.

Rabbit hit the water again. PSSHH!

Nothing happened.

PSSHH! Still nothing.

"Hunh!" said Sungura. "No one is guarding the hole. So I will drink *maji.*"

Sungura leaned over the hole. He put out his two front paws and filled them with cool, sweet water. He closed his eyes, bent his head down, and—

SWSSHH! SNAP! CLICK! Crab's huge claw clamped around Rabbit's paws and held him tight.

It was a long night for Sungura. He begged and he pleaded. He tried to shake off Kaa. He tried to run toward home, away from the water hole. He tried to trick Crab into drinking some of his golden, thick liquid in the gourd. But Kaa just held on tighter and did not listen.

In the morning, when the animals returned to the hole, they found Rabbit sitting quietly. Lion roared with delight.

"So, Kaa. You are not 'only' a crab. Today you are *shujaa*, a hero. You have caught the lazy, lazy rabbit, and now we shall end his days!"

"*Ndiyo*, Simba. Yes, Lion," said Rabbit. "It is best that I end my days here at the water hole."

"I am glad you agree, Sungura. Now, how shall we end your days? What do you fear the most?"

"*Kuruka hewani.*"

"Flying? But you cannot fly, Sungura."

"Exactly. So, please do not throw me up into the air. Elephant, you can trample me. Python, you can squeeze me. Crocodile, you can swallow me. Just please, please, please, do not throw me up into the air!"

Simba smiled. "Of course, we will not. But, if we did throw you into the air, just exactly how would we do it?"

"You would tie all my paws together with the rope around my waist. Elephant would swing me around and around, throw me up into the air, and I would come down, dead."

"*Mfu?*"

"*Mfu*. Dead. Flat, like the grass beneath your feet, Simba."

"That is a terrible thing, Sungura."

"A terrible thing, Simba."

"A terrible way to end your days at the water hole."

"*Ndiyo.*"

"So that is exactly what we will do!"

Lion untied the old, frayed rope from around Rabbit's middle and tied all four of Rabbit's paws together. Only then did he tell Kaa to let go. Lion called for Tembo the Elephant. Tembo took the end of the rope in his trunk. He raised it high into the air, lifting Rabbit off the ground, and began to swing Rabbit around and around and around.

"Oh, please, Tembo!" said Rabbit. "Not so fast."

"Faster, Tembo, faster," roared Lion.

Around and around and around—

"Oh, Tembo, please stop!"

"Do not stop, Tembo, do not stop!"

Around and around and around and—

SNAP!

The rope broke. Rabbit's paws flew out free, and when he fell to the ground, he landed flat on all four of his feet, running. And as he ran he sang:

> Water sweet, water fine,
> Water, water will be mine!

Original Translation

A long time ago there were so many animals. They got together in this one place for a meeting. The meeting was about water because there was no water anywhere. They decided since there was no water, they would dig for water. They all agreed, but the rabbit refused.

When they finished digging the hole, they got the water. Because the rabbit refused to dig the hole, he was told he could not drink the water. So he was trying to find a way to this fishing area and drink that water.

The animals come in the morning and see that the water has been used, but they didn't know who was using the water. So they put up a security. The first time they put monkey as security. The rabbit came down the trails, singing some songs and carrying some honey.

When he came, he hit the water with his stick. The monkey came out. Rabbit said, "Oh, you drink all this dirty water? Why don't you try mine?" The monkey tasted the honey. Monkey said, "Mmmm, it's so sweet. Let me drink yours and you may try mine."

The other animals see that the water is still getting drunk, even though they keep putting out monkeys. So they decide to put the crab as security.

The same thing happened. The rabbit came down the trail, singing some sweet songs, toward the water hole. Then he hit the water. The crab kept quiet, and the rabbit couldn't see him under the water. The rabbit said, "Since there is no one here, I'll drink some water." He got into the water and the crab grabbed him.

He started shouting and shouting, with the crab holding him until morning. All the other animals came and saw who had been drinking their water. They decided to kill him.

The rabbit said, "Why don't you make a big fire. Tie me to a rope and throw me into the air. I will land in the fire."

So the rabbit gave them string that was not strong enough.

The elephant was the strongest, so he was told to tie up the rabbit and throw him into the air. He swung him around and around. He threw him up, the rope broke, the rabbit landed in the bush, and there he went.

Tips on the Telling

Tips

- Research other versions of this story, such as "The Tar Baby" by Dora Lee Newman, published in *North American Legends*, edited by Virginia Haviland (1979). To find additional versions, use *The Storyteller's Sourcebook* by Margaret Read MacDonald (1982); *Index to Fairy Tales*, compiled by Norma Olin Ireland and Joseph W. Sprug; and *A Guide to Folktales in the English Language* by D. L. Ashliman (1987). You will find these books to be invaluable as you do your homework.

- There are many opportunities for audience participation in this story. Before you begin the telling, teach the song so the audience can sing with Rabbit each time. When the frogs sing, you can give cues such as, "the smallest of frogs began to sing in their smallest of voices ..." and so on, for each refrain. You can do the "Be-deep! Go-deep! Now-deep!" on your own, or the audience can join in, if you have taught it to them. The audience can repeat "lazy, lazy rabbit" if you invite them with a hand gesture or head nod. They can answer questions such as, "What was Rabbit carrying in this hand?" "A gourd!" "And in this hand?" "A stick!" They can make the "PSSHH!" sound of the stick hitting water, too. The level of participation is up to you, and it's only by telling the story over and over that you will find out what works best for you.

- The "sweet, thick, golden liquid" is, of course, honey. You can make that obvious with a few knowing looks and smirks from Rabbit, as well as a smacking of lips, licking of fingers, and an emphasis on the word "golden."

- When Rabbit says, "It is best that I end my days here at the water hole," his meaning is ambiguous. Rabbit intends to leave the premises, but Lion's interpretation is that Rabbit knows he will die at the water hole. Again, gently emphasize Rabbit's trickery with an appropriate facial expression or a vocal intonation that implies he has a hidden agenda.

Color Plates

The 15 photographs in this Color Plates section are duplicated from the text. They are presented here to show the beauty of Kenya and its people. The page numbers the photographs appear on are listed at the end of each caption.

Ph.3. The *mzee*, seated in a chair; the *mama*, seated next to him on the ground. (See page 11)

Ph.4. The woman on the left, holding the baby, told the author the story of "Rabbit and Lion."
(See page 12)

Ph.8. Swala Pala the Impala. (See page 23)

Ph.9. The Turkana grandmother and her two friends welcomed the author. (See page 31)
(Photo courtesy of Susan Grant Raymond.)

Ph.11. Two lion cubs. (See page 34)

Ph.15. Wind, grass, and endless skies. (See page 47)

Ph.20. Samwel's sister, in the red dress, told the story of "Monkey's Feast." (See page 61)

Ph.27. Simba wondered who would find water. (See page 86)

Ph.35. Samburu warriors leaping like arrows. (See page 117)

Ph.36. Looking into the eyes of a leopard. (See page 118)

Ph.38. A Samburu *boma*. (See page 119)

Ph.42. Tembo the Elephant. (See page 126)

Ph.43. Hyenas appear "crippled," with hind legs shorter than front. (See page 134)

Ph.49. A baby giraffe. (See page 154)

Ph.52. Mt. Kenya, a spiritual place. (See page 156)

Stories from the Luhya

Who Are the Luhya?

At the end of the sixteenth century, a group of Africans led an exodus of their people from Uganda into western Kenya. Population pressure, political disputes, and illness brought by tsetse flies forced the migration, as did an inherent need to wander, search, and discover. They met with other nomads from the Maasai, Luo, and Ankole tribes. Now, 400 years later, they are settled in the western Province in fertile land that includes five rivers, heavy rainfall, and the lush Kakamega and Bunyala forests.

Like most tribes, the basic social unit of the Luhya was the family. People lived in *litala*, a village, and several villages of the same clan comprised *olukongo*. Each *olukongo* had a leader, *omwami*, who was selected based on his influence within the community. Some of the clans practiced circumcision of the young men. Candidates were secluded for three months, and their food of grain and water was brought to them by a girl especially chosen for this honor. At the end of the seclusion period, the girl was given a small present from the young men. Other traditions among various clans included removing the lower four incisors and the wearing of huge headdresses set on basket bases into which feathers of all kinds were stuck.

The Luhya believed in supernatural powers and asked witch doctors to interpret unusual occurrences. Pebbles determined the guilt or innocence of someone accused of harming another. Each pebble was named after a suspect, and the pebble that most frequently rolled close to the witch doctor revealed the identity of the criminal. Female rainmakers waved a ritual staff toward the sky, boiled a medicinal brew, and demanded gifts from anyone who had annoyed them in order to bring the highly treasured blessing of rain.

Today the Luhya economy is mainly agricultural, with cash crops of maize, cotton, sugarcane, cassava, and tobacco. Livestock are raised for rituals and as bridewealth. The Luhya are well known for their craftsmanship in the arts of pottery and basketry and for playing stringed lyrelike instruments. They are recognized as a hybrid culture, born from and rich with variety.

From My Journal

February 23, 1987

Kisii

I love the markets in Kenya. They are so much more *alive* than the grocery stores and discount stores in the United States. The first thing you notice is the noise—chickens squawking, goats bleating, people bartering and yelling and laughing. Then there are the colors. The produce is carefully stacked and arranged like a patchwork quilt,[31] red tomatoes next to green beans next to orange mangoes. Precarious pyramids of fruit and vegetables look like they could avalanche at any moment, and always there is a "Cowboy" brand can perched on top. Men walk through carrying upside-down live chickens; children chase each other around and through the stalls; women sit patiently and wait for an interested buyer. The smells are a medley of food and humanity—spices, sweat, animal feces, rotten garbage, and sweet fruits.

Ph.31. Goods in a Kenyan market.

But produce is only part of the Kenyan market. There are booths that sell candy bars and sodas. Women have blankets spread out on the ground that display underwear, piles of second-hand clothing, and sandals made from rubber tires. One can buy mirrors, locks, beads, plastic dishes, tin storage boxes, or woven sisal baskets. There are no prices; buying is a matter of bartering, usually beginning with an amount twice the actual value if you are *mzungu* (European, tourist).

After visiting the Kericho Market, we went to the Kakamega Forest to meet Leonard, a friend of Kagathi's and a member of the Luhya tribe.[32]

He took us to the home of an old woman who was delighted to share stories with us. She was clearly recognized by others as *the* storyteller in the village.[33] Her house was mud and stick, with an entry room where we gathered. There was a table where she and Leonard sat, and several stools placed along the walls. Leonard was adamant that the recording be just right, so the story was told in its entirety with no interruptions, then he translated, and then I was allowed to record during her repeat telling.

I remember speaking with Dr. Chris Wanjala of the Literature Department at the University of Nairobi when I first arrived in Kenya. He said some stories must not be interrupted, or you will interrupt the life of the storyteller. I loved that image of teller and story living together as one, and this experiece of collecting stories from the Luhya seemed to exemplify that image.

During the first story a man wandered in, visibly drunk but very friendly, and he eagerly joined in on the telling and the singing. He was loudly hushed more than once, but he would still sing along, obviously very familiar with the story.

Ph.32. Kagathi with his friend Leonard (on the left).

Ph.33. The woman in the flowered dress was the village's best storyteller.

After the stories I took a walk in the forest. There were butterflies everywhere, and it was a dark, dense forest that made me think of Merlin and lost enchantments. I was sorry to leave, for I liked these people. They were friendly, and they were proud of their storyteller.

Ripe Fruit

Retold by Heather McNeil

A long time ago there were eight girls who went into the forest to gather fruit. To find out who was the best at picking fruit, they promised each other they would pick the fruit with their eyes closed.

The girls began to gather *maembe, machungwa, na kokwa*, mangoes, oranges, and nuts. But only one girl, the youngest of them all, kept her promise of closing her eyes. The others, with their eyes open, picked the ripest and the sweetest of the fruit.

At the end of the day the oldest girl said, "Let us walk a mile before we see the fruit we have chosen."

When they had traveled a mile, they checked *maembe, machungwa, na kokwa*. The youngest girl began to cry, for she was the only one whose fruit was not ripe. With her eyes closed she had not seen the green skins. So she told the others, "Wait here for me. I am going back to collect fruit that is ripe."

The oldest girl said, "We cannot wait for you. You will have to walk alone."

"But I do not know the way. I will get lost."

"Then we will put branches along the path. Just follow them, and you will know which way we have gone."

So the girl returned to the fruit trees. She kept her eyes open and filled her basket with *maembe, machungwa, na kokwa*, and this time they were all ripe and delicious. Then she began walking toward home, looking for the branches left by the other seven girls.

Now, the girl did not know that Fisi the Hyena had heard the oldest girl and had removed the branches. He wanted the youngest girl for his wife.

On and on walked the girl, but she could not find any branches to guide her home. She saw only trees and more trees as she went deeper and deeper into the dark forest. Finally, just as *Mwezi*, the moon, was rising, the girl came to a hut, and because she was tired and afraid, she went inside and soon fell asleep.

The hut belonged to Fisi. As he was coming home, he began to sing:

I smell the smell of fruit.
I smell the smell of a lady.
I smell the smell of her perfume.

The girl woke up. She heard the hyena singing outside. She took three nuts from her basket and threw them into the fire.

The hyena continued sniffing and singing:

I smell the smell of fruit.
I smell the smell of a lady.
I smell the smell of her perfume.

All of a sudden the nuts exploded. BAM! BAM! BAM! The hyena ran back down the road, screaming, "There is a devil in my house! A devil in my house!"

Other hyenas came to see what all the noise was about. As they crept toward the house, the girl threw more nuts on the fire. BAM! BAM! BAM! The hyenas began running in circles, howling about devils. The girl climbed onto the roof, then called out, in the voice of a devil, "Any hyena who runs into the forest will die. But any hyena who runs into the water will live."

So, in the dark of night, the hyenas ran into the water—and drowned. The next morning the girl climbed down from the roof and found her way back home, leading the hyena's cattle in front of her and carrying a basket filled with ripe fruit.

Original Translation (Luhya)

There were eight ladies. They went in the forest. They told one another they wanted to go and collect some fruit. When they reached the forest, they said they would pluck this fruit when they had closed their eyes.

When they were in the forest, seven girls plucked some fruit when they had not closed their eyes. But the eighth girl had closed her eyes. And when they left the forest, they told one another, "We should go a distance of about one mile before we see the fruit." Now when they began to check their fruit, seven of them were ripe. But the eighth one, hers were raw. The eighth one began to cry. She told the other seven, "Wait for me. I am going back to collect the ripened ones."

Then the seven ones told the eighth one, "When you come back anytime you see this branch ... that will be the way which I have gone."

A hyena heard. He came and put that branch on his back.

When the lady came, she followed the path agreed on by the seven ladies. She came to a small hut. She entered into this hut. She went upstairs.

When the hyena came in, it began to sing, "I smell another smell of fruit, another smell of a lady, another smell of her perfume." When this girl heard this song, she took three nuts and threw them in the fire. When the nuts exploded, the hyena ran out. It ran out to call more hyenas, that there were devils in the hut.

Many hyenas came in. The girl took a lot of fruit and threw them in the fire again. When she saw that many hyenas had run out, she went on the roof and then called out, "Any hyena who goes into the forest will die. But those who go in the water will live."

All hyenas went into the water and died. Then this lady went out safe.

Original Translation (Kikuyu)

A long time ago there was a girl living in a village called Chuma. There were three beautiful ladies living in this little town. They were all going to fetch water and get wood all by themselves.

One time they met a man. They started laughing at the man. There was one girl who wasn't laughing. She wanted to laugh, but she couldn't laugh with the others. They went home. The next day they went to fetch water. The others started feeling jealous about the one who did not laugh with them. When they fetched water, on the way home they started abusing this one girl.

When they got home, they put away the water. Then they decided they wanted to go and get some fruit. When they got to the tree, they decided to close their eyes and see who could pick more fruit with her eyes closed. But the two decided to open their eyes, and the other kept her eyes closed. When they were done, the two had all the ripe fruit, and the girl who had kept her eyes closed had none, so they decided to try it again. After that, the girl with her eyes closed still had no ripe fruit, but the others had so much.

They told this girl that since she didn't have any ripe fruit, she was not to follow them. They told her the route they were going to take and that they would leave pieces of green grass all along the way.

They knew there was this place with a hyena. When they got to that place, they took another route and didn't leave any more grass. When the girl followed the grass, she ended up where the hyena was, and the hyena got her.

The hyena told the girl, "I'm going to dress you any way you want, and I want you to be my wife." The hyena told the girl, "I'm going to let you go home, but you are not to tell anyone that I am the one who gave you the clothes. If you do tell anyone, I'll come and bring you back."

Since she was dressed up a different way than the others, the girls started asking her why she was dressed this way. The girl couldn't say anything. She went to the uncle whom she really loved. The uncle said, "I'm going to slaughter three goats for you. If you can tell me who did this, I'll give you even more presents."

Then she told him, "Please don't tell the others, because if you tell anyone, the hyena will come and get me and eat me."

After the feast the girl went to fetch water for the uncle. Finally the hyena came and said, "You cannot keep my secret, and I am going to have to eat you." So he ate the girl.

Notes and Tips on the Telling

Notes

I have included both versions of this story that I heard because of their dramatically different endings. The Luhya story seems a version of "Cinderella," where the youngest girl becomes the richest girl because of her bravery and honesty. The Kikuyu story is more like the Charles Perrault version of "Little Red Riding Hood," in which the girl disobeys her mother and is eaten by the wolf.

I found a third version in a small paperback I purchased in Kenya. The book is part of the Elementary English Readers series, published by East African Publishing House, and is entitled *The Girl Who Couldn't Keep a Secret* by Clare Omanga. The story is from Omanga's Kisii background, and it depicts an innocent girl who is tricked by the other girls and then becomes greedy for riches from the hyena. It ends with the following ominous moral: "That night the hyena came and took the girl away. She was never seen again, and her uncle told everybody that they should always keep a secret and allow other people to do the same."

I believe storytellers need to create their own stories, based on all versions available and reflecting the teller's abilities and a consideration of the intended audience. A story should be a weaving of the best.

Tips

- Tell this one straight. No special voices, no large movements, no melodrama. Because the story itself is extraordinary, the telling needs to be the opposite for it to be believable.

- Create your own version of the hyena's song. Try giving it a tune, but if that doesn't feel comfortable, just chant the words, as in the traditional "Fee fi fo fum ..." Repeat the verse to build more suspense. Imagine how the hyena is sniffing and searching for the girl as he chants or sings.

- Before telling this tale, select your audience carefully; I recommend grades 4 and 5, high school, and adults. Listeners should be somewhat familiar with African culture so that they appreciate how unusual it is for a girl, rather than a boy, to be the one who wins.

Stories from the Samburu

Who Are the Samburu?

The butterflies of the desert. People of the white goats. Those who carry the *samburr*, handbag. All are possible meanings of the name Samburu, formerly Burkineji or L'oibor kineji. They call themselves L'oikop, a name of Maasai origin used by the Maasai in a derogatory manner to describe their relatives, the Laikipiak. The term means "those who kill each other," and researchers are mystified as to why the Samburu continue to use such a violent name.

Originally from Sudan, and influenced by contact with ancient Egyptians, the Samburu migrated up the Nile with fellow nomads. They separated from the Maasai, their ethnic cousins, took Mount Ng'iro from the Gulla and Marsabit Mountain from the Laikipiak Maasai, and settled in the highlands between Lake Turkana and the Wuaso Ng'iro River. The Samburu, or Northern Frontier, District, now includes the beautiful and diverse scenery of the Matthews Range, the Ndoto Mountains, meadows, and semidesert.

Author Nigel Pavitt, in his elegant and informative book *Samburu* (1991), describes these people as "a proud and conservative race" and as "traditionalists in a world of change." They are pastoral nomads whose life centers around their cattle and the few crops that can be grown: maize, sorghum, vegetables, and wheat. Milk is the principal food, often curdled with the blood of cattle to create a smoky-flavored yogurt, *saroi*. During the dry season, sheep and goats are slaughtered for meat; soups with roots and barks are also eaten.

The Samburu community is based on friendship and respect, *nkanyit*. A settlement, *manyatta*, comprises from four to ten huts surrounded by a high thorn-branch fence. If timber is not available, the home, *boma*, is made of foliage laid over a framework of brushwood, which is then plastered with cow dung and mud. In the drier regions, mats made from sisal fibers replace the dung. Women are responsible for building and repairing the windowless, single-entrance houses, which are rectangular with rounded corners and approximately five feet high.

The interior features an ever-burning fire in the center, surrounded by stools for visitors. To one side of the reception area is a raised sleeping area for warriors and friends, to the other, a smaller sleeping area for women and children. Behind each house are stock pens for sheep and goats, plus two small enclosures, one to protect kids and lambs, the other for calves.

Among the Samburu, wealth and social status are determined by cattle ownership. Simply put, the more cattle, the better. In addition to meeting basic food needs, cattle are essential to age-grade and marriage ceremonies; without them, community members cannot participate. So vital are cattle that when the Kenya Land Commission imposed a system of grazing schemes in the early 1900s, the Samburu could neither understand nor abide by the stock restrictions. Today, the importance to the Samburu of owning large herds of cattle prevents integration into modern society as their livestock overgraze the land and block development.

Disciplined and orderly, Samburu society is rigidly divided into eight great families. In addition, males are segregated according to age set (females have no age sets, just stages of girlhood and womanhood). According to Pavitt, "initiation into manhood through circumcision is the most significant event in a boy's life." Joseph Campbell, professor of mythology, repeatedly discusses the significance of such initiation rites in *The Power of Myth* (1988), a series of interviews with Bill Moyers. Campbell states, "All children need to be twice born, to learn to function rationally in the present world, leaving childhood behind.... His body has been scarified.... Now he has a man's body. There's no chance of relapsing back to boyhood after a show like that." Pavitt describes the preceding and subsequent events and rituals in excellent textual and photographic detail; only a brief synopsis will be given here.

A young Samburu boy, *layeni*, spends his days tending the herds of goats and sheep. Approximately every fourteen years, a white ox, *lmongo*, is ceremonially slaughtered and eaten as adolescents begin to leave their boyhood behind. *Lorora*, a circular grouping of rectangular houses, is built, each house facing a holy mountain such as Mt. Ng'iro or Mt. Kenya. Initiates are dressed in traditional blackened goatskin cloaks, and they travel from *manyatta* to *manyatta*, singing *lebarta*, a haunting song said to give encouragement to the initiates, *lay-iok loolkilani*. When initiates have returned and the circumcisor arrives, all sharp instruments are blessed with milk. The boys also sprinkle milk into a spring and collect marsh grass for decoration, both traditions symbolizing the strong affinity with their cattle. The milk blessings continue, with mothers sprinkling it at the feet of the initiates and wetting the initiates' hair with it before shaving their heads.

During the actual ceremony of circumcision, initiates are expected to remain calm; a display of fear or pain would disgrace the entire family. The boy would be labeled a coward and could never marry.

The circumcisor, *lakitoni*, performs about one operation per minute. Despite minimal hygiene and the fact that by the end of the morning the knife is dull and the circumcisor is often drunk, complications are unusual. After the operation, the boy is carried into his mother's house, where he drinks cow's blood and milk. The next day he washes himself, and he is now *laibartak*.

Many restrictions govern the new initiate's life. He cannot wash for one month, drink water for two weeks, or stay outside the *manyatta* after sunset. He may not hold any sharp instrument, pick up food with his fingers, or break the bones of any animal he eats. He may not climb trees or wade rivers, kill anything except birds, or quarrel. He spends his days of recovery hunting birds with a bow and blunt arrows; the dead birds are skinned, stuffed with dry grass, and attached to the boy's headband by their beaks.

To become a warrior, *moran*, the initiates must undergo five ceremonies. Each climaxes with the slaughter of an ox or goat, so the ceremonies are called *lmuget*, "the death of many cattle in one place." The last is *lmuget loolbaa*, at which the feasting is carefully orchestrated. Strict rules govern who eats which portion of the meat. The initiate takes part of a broken left hipbone to his mother and promises not to eat meat seen by a married woman. His bird headdress is discarded and trampled by the cattle. He playfully shoots his arrows to the children, symbolizing the end of his childhood.

He is now *lmuran* or *moran*, and his life revolves around his age-mates and his cattle. It is a time of privilege and of exotic habits, including painting the body with red ochre designs and creating elaborate hairstyles of shoulder-length plaits, some of which are fashioned into a "visor." Their independent lifestyle includes considerable freedom with the teen-age girls, *en-toyie*, and frequent displays of their youth and fitness through vigorous dances and leaps. Cloth-ing is unimportant—only a brightly colored loincloth is wrapped around the waist—but ornamentation is vital and includes ivory plugs in pierced ear lobes, beads crisscrossed over the shoulders and chest, and a *simi*, or dagger, hanging exposed on the right side of the body.

The sole responsibility of the *moran* is the safety of the cattle. Long ago, cattle raids were frequent, but now *moran* act more as guards against rustlers and preda-tors. In the dry season they work long hours gathering water for the livestock, and they walk long distances to find the best pastures. The lean warriors will frequently be seen walking across the countryside, arms draped over a spear carried across the shoulders and the red *shuka*, or robe, flapping in the hot winds. They are fearless, arrogant, and have a highly strung tempera-ment that often causes fits, *ndokuna*, which are much like epileptic seizures but are considered a sign of man-liness. They are dedicated to a close companionship with their fellow warriors, always greeting each other with, "*Supa murata*. Greetings, fellow age-mate."

During their years as *moran*, the young men take part in a series of ceremonies that ultimately transform them into elders.

Wedding necklace.

- *Lmuget Lewatanta*, the Ceremony of the Roasting Sticks, when elders give instruction on responsibilities and behavior, and the *moran* begin looking after the cattle.

- *Lmuget Lenkarna*, the Ceremony of the Name, when leaders are chosen from each clan and a new age set name is assigned. The warriors now assume full responsibility for the defense of the tribe.

- *Lmuget Lelaingoni*, the Ceremony of the Bull, when a ceremonial white bull is killed and the *moran* are permitted to marry.

- *Lmuget Lekule E Mbene*, the Ceremony of the Milk and Leaves, performed after the next age set is circumcised and at a time when the cattle are fat. The elders call the *moran* to the central meeting place, *naapo*, to give their blessing. The warriors drink milk, an ox is eaten, and the men are no longer restricted from eating food in front of married women. They are now treated as elders.

When the *moran* become elders, the beads and spears are replaced with a stick and an assortment of hats. Elders spend much of their time sitting in the shade of a tree, discussing a wide range of topics, from gossip to debate. All major decisions must be unanimous, and achieving consensus can take many days. The elders are the disciplinarians and the educators of Samburu society, with the formidable power to impose a curse on those who do not respect their law. They believe the curse will not harm the innocent but will rightfully punish the guilty.

In contrast to that of the important and revered Samburu male, a female faces a much more restricted and conditioned lifestyle. A girl is trained for motherhood as soon as she is able to care for babies and help with chores. She is taught that marriage is an arranged investment, not the result of passion or romance. As a teenager she is allowed to have a lover from the *moran* of her same clan, but there are strict guidelines and limits for sexual activity because pregnancy before marriage is unacceptable. Usually, she will become a bride at around the age of fifteen; her husband will be ten to twenty years her senior and from another clan. She is circumcised on the day of the wedding, and the next day she will walk to her husband's home. He will give her cattle, but the herd will be kept for the son she hopes to bear. Children are her value; to die childless is to be cursed. Her life will be spent raising her children, milking the livestock, hewing and carrying wood, drawing water, building and repairing houses, and preparing food.

The religious beliefs of the Samburu are based on their god, Nkai, or Ngei. They believe he lives in sacred mountains, large trees, caverns, and water springs. Prayers are offered to Nkai for the necessities of life. Sacrifices are also made, such as *Sorio*, held twice a year in every *manyatta*. It is a feast of thanksgiving, at which the blood of a black sheep is mixed with the contents of its stomach and spread over homes and animals.

The Samburu have their superstitions, such as a belief in an evil spirit, Milika. They refuse to count their herd of cattle because that would bring bad luck. Milk must always be put into a container made of a vegetable and must not be boiled nor drunk immediately after being collected. Witch doctors consult stones and other objects in a calabash to solve incurable illnesses and cattle epidemics. *Laidetidetani*, a diviner or dreamer, is the male tribesman who interprets dreams and forecasts rain. *Lais* is the Samburu male who has the power to find things and to bring good or bad luck.

The Samburu do not believe in life after death. Only babies and the very old are buried; others are left for scavengers to eat. If a person dies inside a home, the entire *manyatta* must move to another site, so the old and the sick are taken outside each day. If an infant dies, the child is buried deep inside the house, and the house is burnt to the ground.

For a long time, the Samburu culture has remained intact, resisting change and the influences of modern society. Traditions, designed to unite and strengthen the people, have evolved over hundreds of years and are still practiced, although their origins are forgotten.

However, as more children become educated in schools, the youth are tempted by the materialism they read about and see. They leave for the cities in hopes of making more money. *Moran* perform their dances for tourists, and women offer to have their pictures taken in exchange for soap. Elders, whose word was once law and whose curse demanded respect, now find that the younger generations are questioning their power. Settlements are encroaching upon their territory, and authorities require changes in agricultural practices.

In twenty years, what traditions will remain? And who will tell the stories?

From My Journal

February 16, 1987

Samburu Game Lodge, Samburu National Reserve

Ph.34. A dik-dik.

The game drive today was great fun. The highlight was a pair of dik-diks, tiny and delicate as a whisper.[34] They are the smallest of the antelopes, and Kagathi said they mate for life. "If you kill one, you might as well kill the other."

The giraffes were hilarious, curiously peering at us over the tops of acacia trees. They are the clowns of the savannah. We saw a basking crocodile, herds of elephants, waterbuck, impala, oryx, zebra, ostrich, warthogs, and a flock of vultures dining on an elephant carcass. They crawled inside the bloated body to pluck out bits and pieces of what was once an invincible giant.

When we returned, two Samburu warriors were waiting for me. Earlier in the day, before the game drive, I went to see a group of *moran* (warriors) dance at the Samburu Lodge. I paid my fee, which included the privilege of taking pictures. But I kept my tiny tape recorder hidden.

The performance was intense and macho, with high trilling and low lionlike grunts. They leaped straight up like arrows,[35] very aware of their lean strength and masculine appeal. The Samburu women pretended to be bored with this display, and they would bow and bend, their layers of beaded necklaces bouncing in rhythm. The men would then pretend to become aggravated, and one would charge over to a woman and snap his long ochred hair into her face. She remained aloof and unimpressed.

After the performance I packed my camera slowly, listening to the chatter of the dancers. The other tourists were gone when I felt a tap on my shoulder. I turned to find one of the *moran* pointing at my recorder with his *simi*, a double-edged dagger, and demanding, "Want to hear!" I had fooled no one.

Ph.35. Samburu warriors leaping like arrows.

So I played back what I had recorded, and soon I was surrounded by *moran*, giggling and hooting at themselves on tape. They were very friendly, and each one wanted to be recorded individually, playing the long flute or singing a solo. I managed to express my desire to hear stories, and when Kagathi returned, he arranged for the storytelling after our game drive.

The drive took longer than expected, for we saw so many beautiful animals. When we returned, there in the lobby two of the warriors waited, each standing on one leg, with the other foot resting on the knee of the standing leg, a seven-foot spear held in one hand, their red *shuka* robe so very red and their black skin so very black. They were not pleased with our lateness, and one grabbed my wrist and tapped my watch. We apologized.

At first I was left alone, for Kagathi had to take care of the vehicle. One of the warriors spoke passionately and at great length in broken English to me, and I tried desperately to understand what he was saying about "orés." When Kagathi returned, he explained that this word was "warriors," and the conversation continued in Swahili, Kagathi translating the explanations of Samburu traditions and customs, plus a clever story about why hyena is crippled and spotted.

Now, after dinner, I am waiting to see the leopard feed on the bait left for him in a tree by the Lodge. The night is glorious, with a canopy of stars and a three-quarter moon overhead. There are hundreds of frogs croaking, and every once in a while the monkeys screech as some animal disturbs their peace. The leopard, perhaps?

July 7, 1988

Samburu Game Lodge, Samburu National Reserve

I have looked into the eyes of a leopard.[36]

During our game drive, we saw about twenty-five vans parked

Ph.36. Looking into the eyes of a leopard.

together and assumed the tourists were watching the mother leopard we saw this morning, busy with her three cubs. We waited until most of the vans had left, then drove over to find not Mama Chui, but a very dignified, serene male leopard, tucked in a barren tree about fifteen feet off the ground. We stayed until everyone left, then just stood in silence in the van, eye to eye with Chui as the sun set. "Africa!" whispered Kagathi.

The other highlight of today was collecting stories from the *moran* that I visited with last year. They remembered me, and we all sat in the shade after their dancing and listened to more stories.[37] A tall, thin warrior with a frustrating stutter told stories in Samburu, his friend translated into Swahili, and Kagathi translated into English. So my laughter was a bit off cue by the time I could understand, but we all enjoyed the antics of Ground Squirrel escaping from Lion, and Hyena tricking Baboon. I do not understand why, but I felt completely at home, as if surrounded by old friends. They're not, of course; I barely know them at all. But Kagathi says I understand and learn too quickly for someone who has been only a brief visitor. "You belong here," he said.

After the stories, we celebrated with too many Polaroid pictures. They draped a beaded headdress on me and called me *mama mzungu Samburu*. White Samburu woman.

As I write this, I am in the dining room of the Samburu Lodge. A few feet away is one of the *moran*, the one with the stutter. He is over six feet tall. A red-and-white checked skirt is knotted over one hip; many beads decorate his arms and neck and crisscross his chest. A single feather, like

Stories from the Samburu

a rhino's horn, protrudes from his headdress, and his shoulder-length hair is smeared with ochre, a mixture of herbs, fat, and the red earth of Kenya. Every once in a while he leans against the wall and plays a long black flute with tuneless trills and whistles. He sees me and smiles.

Africa!

February 17, 1987

Maralal

I was given a privilege today. I was invited inside a Samburu *boma*, home,[38] and sat with the *mzee* and his family while they shared stories. It was incredible, like being in

Ph.37. Listening to stories with the moran. (Photo courtesy of Susan Grant Raymond.)

another world and time, so quiet and simple. The *boma* had no windows, and I thought it would be unbearably hot and smoky, with a fire burning in the middle of the floor to cook a pot of maize and beans. But instead it was just cozy and dark; the fire keeps away the flies, and it makes the people smell of earth and smoke. However, I understand that it is part of the reason so many of these people suffer from eye diseases.

The home was made of wood and cattle dung. It had a side pen for the cows if they are threatened by animals or raiding Somalis. Inside was a

Ph.38. A Samburu *boma*.

large wood-slat bed; I was told the man sleeps on the left, and the wife and children sleep on the right.

I sat on the bed next to the wife, who was dressed in her finest to sell maize at the market. She looked so clean and colorful in the brilliant beads and red cloths of the Samburu. There were five children, two cats, the *mzee*, two sons, one wife, Kagathi and myself in the *boma*. I loved the closeness of it all, and how different family members shared different parts of the story, helping each other out.

There was one disturbing image I must record. While Kagathi was visiting with the *mzee*, before the storytelling began, a young girl, about sixteen, stepped in briefly, fully adorned in all her beads and clothes, plus a feather-and-bead headdress. She was shy but curious, and she stood in the doorway, weaving slightly from side to side. Kagathi spoke to her and winced at her reply. Later, he explained that she was circumcised just two days ago and is still recovering. This is a tradition that is strongly discouraged in modern Kenya because of the pain and mutilation. But some of the cultures choose to continue the practice. I cannot begin to imagine her discomfort.

After the storytelling was over, including some tales told by an elderly man who was practically blind and toothless but so obviously respected in his family, Kagathi took us to an overlook of the Great Rift Valley for a picnic lunch.[39] We sat munching cheese and sandwiches,

Ph.39. The Great Rift Valley.

looking down over miles and miles of canyons and chasms, mountains and rivers. Then we returned to the Samburu family and gave them a ride to the market. They were also going to the hospital with an infant who had fallen into the fire and was recovering from a badly burned arm. There is so much we could do to help these people, to help them survive eye diseases, burns, circumcision, and other trials of survival; there is so much we could learn from these people, about respect for elders, family, tradition, harmony with nature, and survival.[40]

After the market, we drove through miles and miles of hot, dry, dusty desert. We saw occasional camels, zebra, waterbuck, impala, dik-dik, and a jackal. Mostly we saw termite hills, red earth, and shrubs. And then all of a sudden we'd come upon a herd of goats and cattle tended by Samburu warriors, spears laid across their shoulders, hands draped over the spears, their bodies adorned with beads, feathers, and the red earth, and their scarlet robes fluttering about them like butterflies of the desert.

Ph.40. There is much we could learn from the Samburu people.

July 20, 1988

Maralal Safari Lodge, Maralal

Here I sit on the grass, overlooking a waterhole at which zebra and impala are drinking. There is a herd of the elusive eland to my left, uncommonly tame and led by a huge bull, grey with age. This place is a  haven, with cedar-lined cabins and a small dining room that overlooks a salt lick where the animals gather. Accommodations are a bit rustic—a generator that is temperamental, so electricity is occasional at best, lukewarm water, and crunchy mattresses that sag with overuse. The staff promises morning tea but does not remember to deliver, and no one can exchange money. But Susan and I are more in tune with Kenya now, and we just learn to change paths.

The drive here to Maralal was uneventful, except for picking up the driver of a broken-down truck carrying dried fish from Turkana to Nairobi. His wife gave him 10 shillings and three pop bottles to exchange, I guess for either petrol or help. He reeked of fish.

When we arrived in Maralal, Susan and I were immediately adopted by two boys, about age twelve, who escorted us around town, pointing out the shop that sells color film, the old lady who makes Turkana dolls, the Samburu women who bead necklaces, the *mzee* who sells dried herbs and grasses for stomach ailments, the market where one can buy *miraa*, an addicting but legal drug that acts as a stimulant when the leaves' stems are chewed. As soon as we returned to the Land Cruiser, the business began. "Madam, you see these bracelets? We sell these to buy what we need for school. You buy so I can go to school? We make good price." About six of these boys surrounded Susan, having quickly learned I visited last year and wanted no more bracelets. They're well-spoken children, proud of their English and knowledge of the United States. "Is Colorado near New York? I have good friend in New York." "Colorado? Is that where cowboys are?" "Headhe (their pronunciation of my name), what do you do in America? You are librarian? With books, many books?" Kagathi says these boys often get sponsors from tourists who are impressed with their cleverness, but I found their answers too slick. "Why aren't you in school today, Jamal?" "Today is day of races. I cannot race, so I am not in school today."

Kagathi took us on a ride up the mountain, intending to let us overlook the Great Rift as we ate our picnic lunches. But the Rift was hidden in clouds. We stood there, just enjoying the heavy silence, when suddenly we heard cowbells. From out of the mist appeared six Samburu children, their cattle, and one warrior. We gave them the remains of our lunches and asked if we could take their picture, but the warrior was adamantly against it. Kagathi said they think it takes their soul, as did the Native Americans. Usually, though, they'll allow it if offered the right price. I believe it is not so much a taking of the soul, but more a taking of pride and often an invasion of privacy. Kagathi said his rear window was broken by a rock thrown by a Samburu warrior who saw one of Kagathi's clients snap a picture without requesting permission. "This is no joke to them," he said. "I once saw a *mzungu* being chased by a warrior waving a *simi* (dagger) over his head." Kagathi rescued the tourist by letting him in his van. I think he should have let the warrior have him. When will tourists learn that taking pictures requires respect for the subject of the photograph, whether it is animal or human?

We never saw the Rift, but the moors were splendid, with a carpet of yellow, white, and purple flowers and the puffs and plumes of fog rolling across. We passed the *manyatta* (village) we visited last year for stories. It looked so peaceful and brought back such pleasant memories of stories told in the sweet smoky smell of their *boma*.

On the way back we visited the house where Jomo Kenyatta was held prisoner before Kenya's independence. It was quite impressive to see the bed where he slept and the desk where he wrote *Facing Mount Kenya*. The museum guide told us that when the British brought him, by airplane, he was blindfolded and did not know where he was. "Then they took off the blindfolds, here in this room, and when he saw Mt. Kenya, he knew he was still in his own country."

July 21, 1988

Maralal

Today began at 6:00 a.m. because Kagathi wanted an early visit to the Great Rift overview. *Chai* (tea) was not ready, so we waited. Then we took the night guard to his *manyatta*. Then we headed up the mountain. Then we had a flat tire. Then we waited while Kagathi replaced it. Then we went back down the mountain because the spare tire did not have enough air, so we couldn't risk going any farther. *Bahati mbaya*. Bad luck.

Down we came, only Kagathi said, with that mischievous grin we know so well, "Surprise *kidogo*." A small surprise. We returned to the night guard's village for a wealth of stories. At least thirty Samburu of all ages came and went during the next hour of storytelling. The people were very friendly, and the stories were excellent. The guard really got into the telling as he translated from Samburu into Swahili, and Kagathi and I could understand the trick or punch line just by watching him jump or cower or stretch.[41] Most of the stories were of Rabbit, and they had definite plots and endings. I paid each teller, plus extra for the translator.

It is such a spiritual feeling for me, sitting among people whose language I do not understand and whose lifestyle I cannot participate in, but whose stories can be shared and enjoyed by everyone. They laugh at each other's stories, and they laugh again when I laugh at the translation. When the story is of warriors, the mood immediately and instinctively changes, becoming somber and respectful. I genuinely believe they are proud to share their stories, and I am proud to receive them.

So now we're back at the cabin, in the midst of a terrific rain, *mvua kubwa*. The thunder rumbles so close the earth trembles. The zebras haven't the sense to get out of the rain, and they stand, soggy and bewildered, at the salt lick. A family of warthogs passed by with two "wartlets." Earlier we were drying laundry in the sun and listening to the doves' mournful cries and the barks of the male impala as he pursued the female he desired. But now it is winter again in Kenya, and the rain is pure and clean.

Ph.41. The guard (on the right) translated from Samburu into Swahili.

Stories from the Samburu

July 22, 1988

Safari Lodge, Maralal

A cold, wet, rainy day. The rain finally stopped late yesterday afternoon, and Kagathi took us to another *manyatta*, where the same man helped translate the stories. The families knew we were coming, so more than thirty had gathered by the time we got to the top of the mountain. One by one stories were offered. The guard discarded some as *hapana mzuri*, not good. Seven different tellers gave us stories, and the stories were very different from the hilarious trickster tales of the morning. These were about warriors and wives and hunting the enemy. Endings were a bit abrupt, as if the translator could hardly wait to get to the conclusion so Kagathi would shout, "*Mzuri sana!* Well done!" and every-one would clap and cheer. Only two were told by men, one of whom was a very tall, somber Ethiopian-looking elder wrapped in a grey wool blanket. His features were very different from the others, looking as eternal as Moses.

The women were hushed and slapped repeatedly by the guard whenever they spoke out of turn. One scowling old woman was dis-missed quite abruptly, and she pouted over to the side with other women sitting on the ground. Another got quite confused or forgetful, and she was berated loudly and soundly. It was difficult for me not to interfere. Another young wife, probably no more than fifteen years old, with a baby strapped on her back, told a revealing story about a barren woman who wants to escape a husband who beats her. After trying to get rid of his two children by his other wife, she is forced to return to the abusive husband. In the stories, these women's self-esteem and value seem to appear in childbearing.

Despite these uncomfortable moments, it was a warm and joyous gathering. The people were very friendly and receptive to us. It was sundown as we left, and huge, pearly clouds filled the blue sky. The eucalyptus trees cast long shadows, and the peace of families gathering was all around the *manyatta* as we drove back down the mountain. "This is the best day of my life," I declared, and Kagathi and Susan laughed, for each day I say the same thing. But this one was special, beginning and ending with good stories and friendship.

Susan and I fell asleep with a crackling fire. Sometime during the night the rains returned, and a hyena howled through the darkness.

Now it is our last full day in Kenya, and, like our hearts, it is heavy and grey. We have been to town, but no one was able to cash our travelers' checks. We lunched, watching the vervets, impala, and zebra. Tomorrow we begin our journey home, and I am trying to pretend that the end is not so near.

Good Luck, Bad Luck

Retold by Heather McNeil

A long time ago, Tembo the Elephant was going to visit his friend.[42] He had heard that his friend was *mgonjwa*, sick. So he filled two gourds with *mafuta*, fat, set the gourds on his back, and down the road went Elephant. Dhon! Dhon! Dhon!

Along came Sungura the Rabbit, hopping down the road past Elephant. Bba! Bba! Bba! "*Hujambo, Tembo!* Hello, Elephant!" Bba! Bba! Bba! "*Unakwenda wapi?* Where are you going?" Bba! Bba! Bba!

Ph.42. Tembo the Elephant.

"I am going to visit my friend who is *mgonjwa*. I am taking him two gourds of *mafuta* to make him strong and healthy again."

"*Mafuta?*" Rabbit stopped. He turned around and hopped quickly back to Elephant. Bba! Bba! Bba! "*Mabuyu mawili ya mafuta?* Two gourds of fat? How kind of you, Tembo! Is it a long journey to see your friend?"

"*Ndiyo*, Sungura. Yes, Rabbit. *Safari nrefu*, a long journey."

"And you will be all by yourself. That will be very lonely, Tembo."

Elephant looked sad. "*Ndiyo*, Sungura. *Peke yake*. All by myself." Suddenly Elephant smiled. "Sungura, why don't you come with me on *safari*?"

"Come with you, Tembo? Oh, I would love to, but—I can't."

"Why not?"

"*Macho yangu.*"

"Your eyes? What about your eyes, Sungura?"

"My eyes are not seeing too well lately, and *safari nrefu* would be very hard for me. I might get lost."

"You will not get lost, Sungura. I will carry you on my back with the gourds."

"Eh, Tembo, you are *huruma*, so kind." Elephant reached out his trunk, wrapped it around Rabbit, and set him on his back. Then down the road went Elephant. Dhon! Dhon! Dhon!

All that Rabbit really wanted was *mafuta*, the rich, thick, delicious fat. His eyes had no trouble seeing the gourds, and he immediately opened one. He ate and he ate and he ate, until his belly was *jaa*, full, and the gourd was *ntupu*, empty.

Then Rabbit called down to Elephant, "Eh, Tembo! My eyes are feeling so badly. Tears are coming into my eyes. Would you give me some leaves so I can wipe *macho yangu*?"

Elephant pulled away palm leaves and handed them up to Rabbit. Rabbit stuffed the leaves into *buyu ntupu*, the empty gourd, while down the road went Elephant. Dhon! Dhon! Dhon!

Rabbit began eating *mafuta* from the second gourd. He ate and he ate and he ate until his belly was *jaa* and the gourd was *ntupu*. Then Rabbit called down to Elephant, "Eh, Tembo! I am so hot and sweaty, sitting up here in the sun on your back. Would you give me a little bit of dirt to sprinkle on myself?"

Elephant dug up dirt from the red earth and handed it up to Rabbit. Rabbit poured the dirt into *buyu ntupu*, while down the road went Elephant. Dhon! Dhon! Dhon!

Just before Elephant arrived at his friend's home, he walked underneath a tree. Rabbit reached up, grabbed a low-hanging branch, and Elephant went on down the road—without Rabbit! Dhon! Dhon! Dhon!

Elephant came to the end of his *safari*. "*Hujambo, rafiki!* Hello, friend! I heard you are *mgonjwa*, so I brought you *mabuyu mawili ya mafuta* to make you well and strong again. Just take the gourds off my shoulders. But be careful of Sungura. His eyes are not good, and he cannot see well at all."

His friend looked up at Elephant's back.

No Rabbit.

He lifted down a gourd and opened it up.

No fat.

He lifted down the second gourd and opened it up.

No fat.

"Tembo, there is no rabbit and there is no fat. You brought me two gourds full of leaves and dirt!"

Elephant was so ashamed and so angry. "I did not travel *safari nrefu* to bring my friend dirt and leaves. I will find that thief, SUN-GU-RA!" Elephant knew he would have to be clever. He put a beautiful necklace on his head and disguised his voice so Rabbit would not recognize him. Then back down the road went Elephant. DHON! DHON! DHON! Into the forest went Elephant. DHON! DHON! DHON! Over to Rabbit's house went Elephant. DHON! DHON! DHON! Elephant stopped.

"SUN-GU-RA!"

A rabbit came out of the house. "Eh, Tembo, what do you want? Why all this stomping and yelling?"

"I want to see the young rabbit who has 'bad eyes' and a full belly."

"Why do you want him?"

"I have something very special to give him."

"There are four of us in this house, but none of us have bad eyes."

"Then I will see the one with a full belly."

"That is not me. My belly is *ntupu. Kwaheri*, Tembo! Goodbye, Elephant. *Bahati mjema!* Good luck!" The rabbit hopped into the forest. Bba! Bba! Bba!

Elephant called out again. "SUN-GU-RA!" Out came another rabbit, but he, too, had an empty belly. Four times Elephant called out for a rabbit to come to him, and it was the last rabbit that had a round belly, tight like a drum.

"Eh, Tembo, what do you want?" asked the fourth rabbit.

"I want the rabbit with the 'bad eyes' and the full belly."

Rabbit took one step back. "Why do you want this rabbit?"

Elephant took one step forward. "I have something very special to give him."

Rabbit took another step back. "What do you want to give him?"

Elephant took another step forward. "I want to give him what he forgot."

"What he forgot?"

"Yes, I already gave him something very special. But he left before he got all that he DESERVES!" Elephant pulled off the necklace.

Rabbit gasped. "And what exactly was the 'something very special' that you gave him?"

"*Mabuyu mawili ya mafuta!*"

"Help! That's me!" The rabbit turned to run for his life, but before his little legs could move, Elephant wrapped his trunk around the rabbit, lifted him onto a branch, and tied him to it with a vine.

"Now, SUN-GU-RA, you are going to get what you deserve. I am going to find a stick, a very large, thick, strong stick, and I am going to beat you! *Bahati mbaya!* Bad luck!" Then down the road went Elephant. DHON! DHON! DHON!

So there was Rabbit, tied to the thorny branch of an acacia tree. He wiggled and squirmed, but the vine held him tight. Finally, he put only his mind to work, trying to think of a plan. And while he was busy thinking, along came Hyena, sniffing and searching for food.

"Eh, Fisi! *Habari gani!* What news?"

Hyena stopped. He looked all around, sure that he had heard the delicious voice of Sungura.

"Fisi! Hyena! Here I am!"

Hyena looked to the right, to the left, in front of him, in back of him. Still no Rabbit.

"Fisi, up here! In the tree!"

Hyena looked up.... Rabbit was in a tree!

"Sungura, what are you doing up there? Do you think you are a monkey?"

"Tembo tied me up here."

"Why would he do that?"

"Because I did not want what he was going to give me."

"What was he going to give you?"

"*Mabuyu mawili ya mafuta.*"

"You refused two gourds full of fat? Why would you do such a foolish thing?"

"Because I do not deserve them. I told him he should give them to someone else, someone very hungry. But he would not listen to me. He tied me here and has gone home to get the gourds of fat. It is too bad he will not give them to someone who wants them."

"Sungura, I want them!"

"You do?"

"*Ndiyo*, yes, I really do. I will eat them for you!"

"Oh, Fisi, you are *huruma*, so kind. We will just put you here in my place, and when Tembo returns, you tell him to give *you* what he was going to give *me*."

So Hyena jumped up and grabbed the end of the vine with his teeth. He pulled until the vine broke and Rabbit fell free to the ground. Then Rabbit lifted Hyena up, and Hyena tied himself to the branch with another vine.

"*Asante sana*, Sungura! Thank you very much, Rabbit!"

"Oh, no, Fisi. It is I who should thank you. *Bahati mjema!* Good luck!" And Rabbit hopped back into the forest. Bba! Bba! Bba!

Hyena waited, his mouth drooling as he thought of all that rich, thick, delicious fat. Finally, he heard Elephant coming down the road. DHON! DHON! DHON! Elephant stopped and stared at Hyena.

"Eh, Fisi, what are you doing here? Where is Sungura?"

"I spoke with him, and he said he did not deserve what you were going to give him. So I set him free."

"YOU DID WHAT?"

"I set him free. But now I am here in his place because I really want what you were going to give him. I think *I* deserve it."

"You do? Then I will give you what I was going to give Sungura. *Bahati mbaya*, Fisi! Bad luck, Hyena!"

And Elephant began beating Hyena with the stick.

Original Translation

A long time ago, Elephant went to visit his friend. The elephant got two gourds full of fat. On his way, he met with Rabbit.

The rabbit asked the elephant, "Hey, my friend, where are you going?"

The elephant said, "I am going to visit my friend. I heard he is sick."

So the rabbit told the elephant, "If you are going there, I can accompany you. My eyes are not feeling too good, so you can carry me."

The elephant told the rabbit he could climb onto his back. So the rabbit climbed onto his back.

The rabbit really wanted a ride so he could eat the fat in the gourds. When he got onto Elephant's back, he started eating the fat until one gourd was empty.

The rabbit told the elephant, "My eyes are feeling so bad. The tears are coming into my eyes. Can you give me some leaves so I can wipe them?" Rabbit put the leaves into the empty gourd.

Rabbit began eating the fat in the second gourd. When he finished it, he told the elephant, "I am so sweaty. If you could just give me a little bit of dirt so I can sprinkle it on myself." When he got the dirt, he filled the second gourd.

When the elephant was just about to get to his friend, he had to pass under these branches. One was very low. The rabbit grabbed one of the branches and was left hanging there as the elephant went on.

When he got to his friend, he kneeled down and he told his friend, "I've just come to visit you because I heard you were sick. I've brought you some fat. Just take it off from my shoulders, please. But don't touch the rabbit. His eyes are not well, and he is very sick."

The second elephant keeps on looking, but there is no rabbit. Then they opened the gourds to eat the fat. One was filled with sand, and the other was filled with leaves.

The elephant was so ashamed after traveling all that way to help his sick friend. So he said, "I am going to go look for the rabbit." He took off.

He put this beautiful necklace on his head so the rabbit wouldn't recognize him. He went to the forest and screamed, "Rabbit, come here!"

A rabbit came out of the forest and asked what he wanted.

"The young rabbit who has bad eyes. Have you seen him?"

Buyu—a gourd fat container.

Good Luck, Bad Luck

"No, I haven't seen him. There's only four in our house, and we all have this red mark on our forehead."

The elephant called four times. The rabbits keep on saying, "No, we don't know this rabbit with the bad eyes." The last rabbit asked the elephant, "Hey, what did you give him?"

"Fat."

The rabbit said, "That's me!"

The elephant grabbed him and tied him to a tree. The hyena came. The elephant had gone to get sticks to beat the rabbit. The hyena asked the rabbit, "Why are you tied here?"

The rabbit said, "I am tied here because I won't eat the elephant's fat."

The hyena said, "I am going to untie you, and you tie me, because I really want the fat. I don't fear this fat. I'll eat it all." The hyena untied the rabbit and the rabbit ran away.

The elephant came back and asked the hyena, "Who are you?"

"It's me, Hyena. I met Rabbit here, and he said he was afraid of what you were going to give him. But I am not afraid. I really want what you were going to give him."

The elephant said, "Oh, so you want it? I will give it to you!" And he began beating the hyena.

Notes and Tips on the Telling

Notes

- Once again, this is a story clearly linked to a Bre'r Rabbit story from Joel Chandler Harris. "A Dollar a Minute" tells how Bre'r Fox finally catches Bre'r Rabbit stealing his peanuts and has him hanging in a tree. But the rabbit convinces Bre'r Bear to take his place so the bear will earn "a dollar a minute" for keeping the crows out of the peanut patch. It is fascinating to me the elements that appear, over and over again, in stories throughout the world. The more I read and listen, the more I realize that it is through our stories we can understand the humor, gentleness, strength, and desires of us all.

- Quite frankly, I have no idea why the first rabbit says, "we all have this red mark on our forehead" in the original translation. I would assume it is an indication of a particular age set, but I'll have to wait for my next trip to Kenya to find out!

Tips

- You might want to explain that eating fat (as well as using it for cooking) is a fairly common dietary supplement in parts of Kenya where they do not have the variety of foods we are used to.

- Use audience participation whenever it seems appropriate to you. The sounds of Elephant walking and Rabbit hopping are easy ones to encourage. Listeners can use voices only, or foot stomps and slight body hops as well. Just remember that you must set the controls; explain before the story that each sound is done three times, or by certain parts of the audience, or following a particular gesture from you. Young children will love the stomping and hopping but need to know when to stop.

- Be sure to change Elephant's voice when he is trying to find the right rabbit. As far as I'm concerned, the sillier the voice, the better.

- Rabbit does not recognize Elephant until the necklace is removed. Then the tension and fear should be immediately obvious when Rabbit loses all his self-assurance. It returns, of course, when he comes up with a plan to trick Hyena.

- Hyena is stupid because of his greediness. Have fun with that through voice and facial interpretations.

- *Bahati mjema!*

Hyena and the Moon
Retold by Heather McNeil

Hyena is a thief, and he has always been so. Hyena is also crippled, hind legs shorter than front legs.[43] But he has not always been so.

Long ago Hyena's legs were all the same. He did not hump and slink across the savannah as he does today. He would trot and prance, run and dance, proud of his speed and courage, proud of his cleverness.

Ph.43. Hyenas appear "crippled," with hind legs shorter than front.

But there was one hyena who was not so clever. His name was Fisi, and he was handsome, with fur the color of honey. He was fast, and he ran with the hot winds that tossed the red oat grass.

Fisi was also a lazy hyena. He never hunted, but let Chui the Leopard and Simba the Lion do the work of stalking and pouncing and killing. Then Fisi would sneak in close and run away, with the meat clenched tightly in his mouth. Fisi would laugh at his cleverness.

Stories from the Samburu

But Fisi was not so clever. There came a time of drought. No rains fell for many months. The water holes were deserted because there was no water, and when there is no water, the animals die.

All the animals were hungry, including Fisi. He no longer danced and pranced, but prowled and howled his way through the grass that scratched like dry fingers. He and the other hyenas continued to steal from Simba and Chui, running off into the night and laughing. But their laughter was dry, too, and died quickly.

One night Fisi's belly was grumbling and rumbling louder than ever. He tried to ignore it by bragging about his cleverness.

"Oh, Fisi, you are not so clever," said another hyena. "You are not even clever enough to fill your own belly. Every day you grow thinner, like all of us. The only one who grows round and full is the moon."

Fisi looked up at Mwezi, the moon. She was indeed round and full, and it made Fisi's mouth water to see the moon's bright richness.

"If only we could grow as she grows," Fisi thought. "If she were in our bellies, then we would be strong like the moon. If only...."

Suddenly Fisi began to laugh. "Eh! I am so clever!" He called together all the other hyenas. "I know how we can fill our stomachs. We will climb up to the moon! I will break off pieces to feed to you, and we will eat until our bellies are round and full like beautiful Mwezi."

"Fisi, you are a fool. How can we climb up to the moon? And even if we could, Mwezi would see us coming, and she would hide. Mwezi sees everything."

"Then we will cover ourselves with the branches of acacia trees," Fisi said. "We will make a tower of hyenas, standing on each other's shoulders. The tower will reach all the way to the moon, and then I will be able to break off pieces of Mwezi to feed to everyone."

The other hyenas laughed. But all night Fisi talked about the moon's power and beauty, and the more he talked, the more the others listened. They looked at the moon standing so proud in the sky, and they knew they wanted her strength.

So the next day all the hyenas gathered acacia branches. They covered themselves, but no matter how careful they were, the thorns

Hyena and the Moon

pricked and poked and jabbed and stabbed.[44] It was even worse for them when they began to build the tower of hyenas, climbing on each other's shoulders, higher and higher toward the moon.

"Ouch! Be careful! You are standing on my nose!"

"Get your paw out of my ear!"

"I can't see! Your tail is covering my eyes!"

Fisi watched from the ground. "*Nyamaza!* Be quiet! Mwezi will hear you!"

Finally all the hyenas were piled on top of each other, and Fisi began his long climb to the top.

"*Haraka haraka!* Hurry, hurry, Fisi!"

"We are hungry! Bring back plenty of the moon for us to eat."

"I can't see!"

This time it was not because of someone's tail that the hyena could not see, but because the moon suddenly disappeared behind a cloud. The savannah was bathed with darkness.

"I told you," Fisi said. "You scared Mwezi with all your loud foolishness. Now we will have to wait until she returns."

So they waited, trying to muffle their whimpers of pain and fear. And as they waited, the tower of hyenas began to weave back and forth, left to right, back and forth, left to right....

Ph.44. Acacia thorns.

Stories from the Samburu

Then three things happened at the same moment:

Moja. One. Mwezi slipped out from behind the cloud where she had been hiding and bathed the savannah with light.

Mbili. Two. Fisi reached the top of the tower and stretched out one eager paw to grab a piece of the moon.

Tatu. Three. The legs of the hyena at the bottom of the tower began to tremble, and quiver, and shake.... "*Saidia!* Help!" His legs collapsed, and the tower crashed to the ground, one hyena tumbling after another. Bumping, sliding, rolling, clawing, and bouncing, the hyenas fell on the trees and thorns, the hard, dry earth, and each other.

When it was all over, there was one brief moment of complete silence as the animals of the savannah saw what had happened under the light of the moon that night. Then the hyenas crawled off into the bushes. Many of them had broken legs. Their fur was torn, and they howled in pain as they humped their way into the shadows to lick their wounds.

So it is even today. Hyena is crippled, hind legs shorter than front legs, and he humps through the red oat grass. His fur is spotted with the scars of his foolishness.

But the children of Fisi still steal from Chui and Simba. They clench the meat tightly between their jaws and run away into the night, laughing at their cleverness.

Original Translation

A long time ago there was this hyena which had a bad leg. It saw the moon. It called all the other hyenas, and they gathered together. He thought the moon looked like something good to eat. He wanted to jump and take it and eat it. They stood on each other's shoulders so the one on top could reach the moon and just pull it down. But the one which was on the bottom, it got very heavy. They all fell down and broke their legs. After they broke their legs, they all left, they left one another, limping. When they went out, they gave birth, and the young ones also had deformed legs.

Tips on the Telling

Tips

- The main thing to remember in telling this story is to take your time! Build the suspense just as Fisi builds the tower.

- Read about hyenas. Watch them in a zoo, if possible. (Better yet, visit Kenya!) Hyenas aren't really the scavengers they were once thought to be, but are actually strong hunters themselves, as well as thieves. They do "hump" and their howls can sound like eerie laughter in the African night.

- If necessary, prepare your listeners for this story with a few facts. For instance, you might want to describe the long thorns on acacia trees so the audience better appreciates the pain of the hyenas. Make sure everyone is familiar with hyenas. You might need to explain predators and scavengers. But make this introduction brief, or you'll lose your audience.

- Remember not to get overly concerned with memorizing my words. After reading the story several times, just tell it to yourself in your own words. Use the Swahili only if you feel comfortable with it; otherwise, leave it out. Then practice, practice, practice. Create a rhythm and pattern that is your own.

- I really had to expand this story; the original translation is hardly more than an outline. It helped to visualize this one as I wrote it, as it does whenever I tell it. Imagine the thin, slinking hyenas prowling about, looking for food. Imagine the savannah bathed in moonlight or silhouetted in darkness. Imagine a tower of hungry hyenas and the fear and trembling they are trying to suppress. My favorite image is one I have of the expressions on the other animals' faces when the hyenas come tumbling down to the ground. Visualization by the storyteller is extremely important in order for the audience to "believe and receive" the story. Imagine!

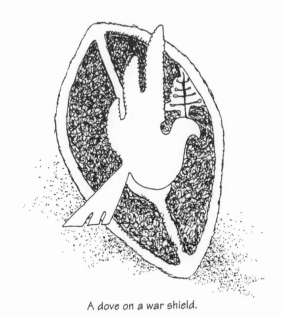

A dove on a war shield.

Hyena and the Moon

Last Days

From My Journal

March 6, 1987

En route to London from Nairobi

My last day ended spendidly on a game drive at Nairobi National Park. At first we saw only the usual (can't believe I'm saying that; it's like having filet mignon every day, until it's "the usual")—giraffe, ostrich, and zebra in the distance, plus an occasional warthog on its knees eating grass or running ahead of us down the road, tail sticking straight up like a periscope. About 5:30 we spotted three eland on the hillside across from us and stopped to try to get a picture. Suddenly, quietly, Kagathi said, "There are lions, Heather, just for you."

It was a lioness with cubs, and she was hunting. For the next hour we watched her stalk the eland. A master at the art of patience, she inched her way up the hill, flattening herself into the grass, gold in gold. Sometimes only the tips of her ears were visible as we followed her slow progress through our binoculars. The eland grazed on, oblivious to their possible doom. Suddenly a bushbuck crashed through the bushes, evidently having caught the scent of the lion. The eland became skittish, their black and sable heads jerking up and over their shoulders, looking for the trouble. The lioness froze, taut and invisible in the rippling grass. Eventually the eland relaxed again and returned to grazing. The lioness crept closer ... closer ... closer. But when she finally moved to kill, all her patience and strength proved useless. She charged out of the grass, the eland bolted into the bushes, there was a snapping and crackling of branches, and all three eland emerged from the other side, unharmed. We drove around to see if we could find the frustrated huntress. She stood alone, gazing off across the savannah, her sides heaving and her mouth hanging open with exhaustion. Then she ambled off, swollen teats hanging low, her body set to pursue another prey.

Then we went in search of the only one of Kenya's "Big Five" that I have not seen—the black rhinoceros. We found a pair grazing across the gully, silvery grey as dusk began. We just sat and watched, and Kenya gave me a glorious final sunset.

Now I'm trapped in a plane on the way to London. I feel totally misplaced, not "where I should be," as Isak Dinesen said so well.

In Kenya, the sun is rising. This is the best time of day, when the dust is settled, the air is cool and fresh, and the animals are resting after a night of hunting for some and death for others. In the cities people are crowding themselves into *matatus*, a few extras always hanging out the back doors of the buses and the tops so overloaded with mattresses, food, and boxes that the vehicles often lean precariously to the side. The markets will open soon, with the piles of neatly stacked pawpaw, potatoes, onions, and oranges. There will be cans of dried beans nestled into mountains of lentils or peas, and there will be chickens running loose, sometimes for their lives.

In the city homes, children will be putting on their school uniforms, and fathers will go off to work in shops and factories. In the villages, children will be gathering herds of goats and sheep to tend, and fathers will gather to chew *miraa*, drink beer, and settle disputes. Everywhere the mothers will begin their day of carrying, plowing, scrubbing, hauling, nursing, cooking, planting, and mothering.

I wonder how I will answer the question, "How was your trip to Kenya?" They will expect me to explain all the diversity and beauty in a few moments. There are so many visions I will always remember, from the black-faced vervet that leaped onto our breakfast table and snatched away the butter, to sitting in the shade of a tree while Samwel nervously tossed a red tree fruit from hand to hand as he translated his sister's story about Hyena. But the vision that is Kenya most for me is driving across endless miles of desert, the dust billowing like red smoke all around us. And then, suddenly, we hear bells, and a herd of cattle and goats appears, with a lone warrior walking among them, his arms hanging on the club across his shoulders, his red *shuka* swaying loosely, and his ochred hair glistening in the heat of the day.

July 24, 1988

Safari Lodge, Maralal

Susan asked if I would travel to places other than Kenya for stories. "I can't imagine you anywhere but Kenya," she said.

Neither can I.

Contradictions and Conclusions

As I read my journals of four and five years ago, I find I have forgotten what made Kenya difficult and remember only what made the country comfortable for me. But then that is why women are willing to have more than one baby, and mountain climbers plan for the next conquest. We remember selectively.

For instance, I forgot how Kenya is a country of contradictions. In the markets, food was more carefully and colorfully displayed than in any American grocery store. Carrots were "teepeed," tomatoes were arranged in precarious towers, and rhubarb was artistically hung upside down, red stem leading to a fan of green leaves. But the sanitary conditions were appalling. Goats rambled in and out, flies were everywhere, and unidentifiable decomposing garbage covered the ground.

In the tourist lodges, the waiters were some of the finest I have ever seen. Napkins were crisply folded, food was served with a clever manipulation of fork and spoon, back to back, and tea came in individual pots with miniature spoons and cream pitchers. But the bathrooms were ignored. Often there was no toilet paper, no soap, no towels, and the toilet was stopped up.

Another Kenyan contradiction involved their dealing with money. They certainly wanted it, and needed it, but exchanging currency was frequently an ordeal of endurance. From my journal of July 22, 1988:

> Lodges never seem to have enough money, banks close at 2:00, and hotels won't exchange unless you're staying there. Today, the bank didn't know what the current exchange rate is because the phones are out due to rain. We were told to come back "midday." When we returned, we were told to come back tomorrow. On Saturday? I explained we were leaving in the morning and needed money for food and tips, but he didn't seem to care. This town will do without our money.

My safari was not always easy. But my belief was that every change of plans, every flat tire, every delicate situation would just add to the *story* of my adventure. And so they did.

February 23, 1987

Maasai Mara National Reserve

We left early today because Kagathi was concerned about reports of bad roads due to rain. By 9:30 we were seriously, unconditionally, hopelessly stuck in mud.[45] We piled up branches, dug out wheels, rocked the van, all to no avail. Kagathi headed back down the road to get help while D. and I did what we could with Swiss Army knives and hands. Two Maasai warriors and women came along. The men just watched, remaining aloof and amazed. (Staring at tourists stranded on the roadside is a common form of entertainment for the people of Kenya.) The women

Contradictions and Conclusions

Ph.45. Hopelessly stuck in mud.

were helpful and pleasant, and they immediately sloshed into the mud with us. When we were all knee-high in the slop, and I was complaining about our dilemma, one of the women straightened herself, looked at me, and said, "God is great."

July 24, 1988

En route to Nairobi from Maralal

I can't begin to describe how frightened we were by the river that used to be the road, and the mud puddles that turned out to be craters, and the sliding into the bank, and the possibility of tipping over as we inched our way past a truck stuck in the middle of the road. "Oh, you can't possibly get by," said the British owner. But Kagathi studied the surroundings, and off we went. He is an excellent driver, with quick, strong reflexes. I call him *mawi*, the rock. During one plunge into a hole that sent a sheet of muddy water over the windshield, I gasped, and Kagathi said, "What's wrong?"

"Nothing," I squeaked, my knuckles white on the door handle. "I'm just breathing." I turned and looked back at Susan. Her arms were stretched to each door, her eyes were wide as silver dollars, and she wasn't breathing.

February 25, 1987

Mara Serena Lodge, Maasai Mara National Reserve

During the evening game drive, we came upon a male lion, alone and dying beneath an acacia tree. He was emaciated and covered with flies, his paws lay bowlegged in front of him, and his tongue lolled out the side of his mouth. Kagathi said, "Nature is doing its work."

February 26, 1987

Old Stanley Hotel, Nairobi

Trading and bartering requires a bit of creativity and a lot of willpower. The salesman starts with an outrageous price, usually mumbled softly or scratched onto his arm. "But for you, a special price," and he'll knock off 50 shillings. Then the customer offers a price, usually half of the original. You can either continue haggling over shillings, or they'll ask, "What you have to trade? Tee-shirt? Watch? Maybe your necklace?" The Maasai today wanted the shirt I was wearing because it was red.

February 28, 1987

Taita National Park

We tried for stories from the Maasai but had no luck. I paid 500 shillings ($30) to get into the village; the *mzee* was taking money right and left from tourists. The admittance fee allowed me to take pictures,[46] but the people were uncooperative, only interested in selling their bracelets. The women clawed all over me, refusing to accept my refusal. I finally had to put the bracelets down in the dirt and walk away.

The people were filthy and absolutely covered with flies. The children had flies all over their faces and in their mouths. The women were aggressive and pushy, the children kept tugging at my sleeves, begging for money or a pen, and the smell of cow dung was overpowering. The *mzee*, wearing a grimy Australian bush hat, invited us into his *boma*, where the flies were a bit fewer in number. It was like the Samburu home but much dirtier, with potato peelings on the floor and cockroaches crawling on the walls. Kagathi tried to explain what we wanted, but the *mzee* had no stories. We left.

Contradictions and Conclusions

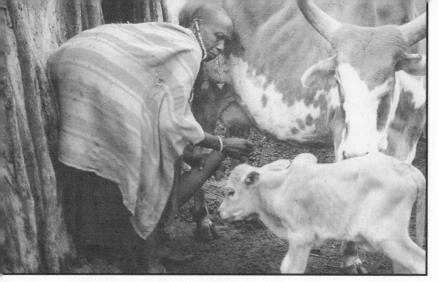
Ph.46. A fee allowed me to take photos like this.

February 15, 1987
Naro Moru River Lodge

We awoke this morning to an inch of cold water on the bathroom floor, due to a leaky shower.

February 23, 1987
Kisii Hotel, Kisii

Our hotel was very atmospheric in its shabbiness. We had a cottage overlooking beautiful gardens, but most of the lights didn't work, the toilet wouldn't flush, there was only one towel, and the beds had no springs.

July 24, 1988
Kisii Hotel, Kisii

Our last day began very early with another cold sponge bath by flashlight, because the generator is more off than on.

February 18, 1987
Sarova Lion Hill

The hillside behind our lodge caught on fire, and for the past three hours people have been standing by with packed luggage, watching flames shoot over the hill. The staff did a great job of keeping people from panicking. It was interesting to see what people grabbed to take if we

Contradictions and Conclusions

were evacuated. D. and I knew we couldn't handle all our luggage, so I carried my tapes, camera bag, and journal. In the midst of all the pandemonium, I remembered to swallow my weekly anti-malaria pill. A fellow tourist laughed and said, "Well, you might burn to death, but at least you won't have malaria!"

February 21, 1987

Sunset Hotel, Lake Victoria

The day we had a picnic overlooking the Rift Valley, we never got to a bathroom from 7:30 a.m. to 4:00 p.m. Kagathi simply stepped off into the bushes, but D. and I were too green to the experience of the bush to take a chance. Later, we got to laughing about the image of creeping off into the bushes, crouching, and then suddenly being surrounded by baboons. "Or, worse yet," D. said, "there would be kids appearing from nowhere, like they do, with hands outstretched, yelling, 'Shilling? Sweet?' Or some trader shoving bangles and carvings in your face, saying, 'I make you good price. You my first customer.' "

February 27, 1987

Amboseli National Park

I have left so much money in this country, and not just from buying musical instruments and artifacts, but because of being flustered with change and exchange. I think I just left a $.67 tip for a $.42 beer.

July 7, 1988

Samburu River Lodge, Samburu National Park

We stopped at the market in Isiolo. It was fun and colorful, until Kagathi told me to say a word that sounded like "ejok" to an old Turkana woman walking toward me. It was supposed to mean "hello," but maybe I mispronounced the greeting, or maybe she dislikes tourists. Anyway, she immediately attacked me, demanding money, grabbing at my clothes, and hitting me. Three Meru men hustled me out safely to the van. Kagathi explained that the woman was probably high on *miraa*.

July 9, 1988

Tea Hotel, Nakuru

About ten miles from Nakuru a tire began falling apart. We had no spare because that had been used to replace the flat we found when we loaded in the morning. So we wobbled along slowly, and every once in a while there would be a loud explosion as another chunk of tire went flying, until we got down to no treads at all. Then Kagathi drove from station to station, trying to find the tires he wanted. "Can't you make a few calls?" Susan asked. "Oh, no, this is not like America," he answered. "Here you have to struggle."

These are all stories, retold here so that *all* I saw, heard, felt, smelled, touched, and learned in Kenya will be remembered and passed on. Every day memories return, and I am there again. I remember

... being offered a bowl of plums and passion fruit, hurriedly picked by Timothy, the Akamba boy still recovering from malaria.

... standing by myself on the shore of Lake Nakuru at sunrise, surrounded by hundreds of flamingoes, storks, and pelicans.[47] Their beating wings caused such a roar, it sounded like a train. And the colors!—white mist on the blue mountains, pink flamingoes, yellow sand, green water, and the rose of dawn.

Ph.47. Lake Nakuru at sunrise.

... laughing at baby elephants learning how to use their trunks. They frequently miss their mouths or smack themselves on the head.

... shouting for joy as I stood in the back of the van and we raced down the road, goshawks diving and soaring all around us.

... touching the armored hide of a white rhinoceros, protected and tamed by guards.

... snorkeling amid the wildlife of the coral reefs along the Mombasa coast. I saw tiny sea snakes, a brown and yellow moray eel, a huge ruffled snake, an angelfish with brilliant blue-and-yellow stripes, and tiny iridescent blue fish by the hundreds. Sea urchins everywhere.

... gasping in amazement when Mt. Kiliminjaro suddenly escaped from the clouds and rose in front of me, a massive white-capped giant.[48] There were elephants bathing in the red dust at her feet, and there was a rainbow.

... emerging in the mornings from the white cloud of mosquito netting. It's like being a snake shedding its skin.

... laughing at the clumsy antics of lion cubs pulling on their father's tail and at baby giraffes who have more skin than their skeletons can hold.[49]

Ph.48. Mt. Kiliminjaro, a massive, white-capped giant.

Contradictions and Conclusions

Ph.49. A baby giraffe.

... noticing the irony of a sign at the check-in desk of a lodge: "The management is not responsible for lost valuables. Please leave your valuables with the management."

... sitting around a huge campfire after a candlelit dinner of roast lamb, yorkshire pudding, and lemon meringue pie at Cottar's Camp, truly heaven on earth. Sparks rose and disappeared among the stars, and we watched bush-babies munching watermelon left for them in a tree. Everyone spoke in whispers, awed by the darkness and vastness of the Maasai Mara. When we were ready to return to our "bungalow," a Maasai warrior appeared from out of the black night to escort us and protect us, spear in hand. My sleep was interrupted when "Number One," the lion with the biggest mane, prowled through camp, coughing and grunting.

... Above all, listening to the stories of Rabbit, Hyena, drought, famine, hunters, warriors, Lion, Baboon, men, women, children, wizards, forests, deserts, mountains, death, life.

As we gather stories, as we listen to the tellers who continue the tradition of passing on the lessons of another time and another world, we must remember that it is all part of The Story. Those of us who open ourselves to "believe and receive" must pass on all that gives life to the tale. We must know the creators, the history, the characters, the setting, the colors and sounds and smells of that story. "Move right in and live in your story," says my mother. Do your homework, I say. And when you have dressed yourself from the inside out, with the skeleton, blood, and skin of the story, then you are one of the few who can say, "I am a storyteller, and I have a story to tell."

July 3, 1988

Naro Moru River Lodge, Mt. Kenya National Park

I am home, back in Kenya. In some ways, I never left.[50]

Kagathi led Susan and me on an all-day walk up Mt. Kenya. We began at 10,000 feet and progressed slowly, cautioned by Kagathi to remember the combination of the change in altitude and our jet lag.

The forests of this sacred mountain are "lovely, dark and deep." Pools of light shimmer through the trees, highlighting the greens of velvet moss, swaying ferns, and massive cedars. It is a place of

Ph.50. Back in Kenya. (Photo courtesy of Susan Grant Raymond.)

magic, especially when you remember that you are walking in the kingdom of elephants and cape buffalo.

The second level is heath, with lobelia, flowers, tussock grass, thistles, and sagelike bushes. Tussock grass grows in soft, feathery clumps. It feels like the coarse hairs of a horse's tail, but it looks like soft, swaying sea anemones pillowing the heath.[51] There are buttercups, neverending flowers, red fire pokers, St. John's wort, and cabbage rubilia. The latter holds pools of water in its flowered center and closes at night to sleep.

Kagathi was in his prime, snapping off branches to smell and leaves to rub. He identified a myriad of birds—hillchat, francolin, paradise flycatcher, green hoopoe, mountain buzzard. We came upon a troop of baboons, and I saw a bushbuck fleetingly. There were colobus monkeys, their black-and-white-plumed bodies diving off the branches high above and plummeting to another branch far below. One missed and crashed to the ground but quickly ran back up into the trees, unharmed but surely embarrassed.

For many of the ethnic groups in this country, Mt. Kenya is a spiritual place, the place where life began and the Creator resides.[52] Kagathi walked gently on the earth of this mountain, respectful of his people's stories of Gikuyu and Moombi.

Contradictions and Conclusions

Ph.51. Susan Grant Raymond surrounded by tussock grass.

Ph.52. Mt. Kenya, a spiritual place.

Contradictions and Conclusions

Upon our return to Naro Moru Lodge, we spoke with Francis, who works at the reception desk. He is a storyteller:

Hyena was hunting for food. A huge rock fell on him, and Hyena could not move.

Along came Rabbit. "Eh, Hyena, what is wrong with you? Why are you under that rock?"

"I need your help, Rabbit. Please come and set me free." So Rabbit helped Hyena and set him free.

"Thank you, Rabbit," said Hyena. "And now I am going to eat you."

"Oh, very well," said Rabbit, "you may eat me. But first, I do not understand—how was it that you got caught under that rock?"

"It was like this," and Hyena let the rock roll back on top of him. He could not move. "Do you understand now?"

"Yes, I understand," laughed Rabbit. And Rabbit ran away, free.

"The more I learn about how things are," said Francis, "the more I learn that life is like our stories."

And so it begins.[53]

Ph.53. And so it begins, one generation to the next. Kagathi and his daughter, Winrose Waithira Kagathi.

Glossary

The *highlighted* words used in the stories are Swahili; their pronunciations and meanings are given here. The *highlighted* words included in the sections about the various cultures are in the groups' own languages and are taken from written resources that did not offer pronunciations. Because I am not familiar with those languages, their pronunciations will not be given here.

Swahili is a Bantu language, and it incorporates words from many sources, including Arab and Indian settlers and traders, Portuguese and German colonists, and the English.

I have used *Swahili: A Foundation for Speaking, Reading, and Writing* by Thomas J. Hinnebusch (1979) as a resource for the following pronunciation guidelines:

Swahili	As in English
a	*ah*
e	s*ay*
i	b*e*
o	g*o*
u	*too*
f	*f*ew
g	*g*oat
j	*j*ob
m	Often a prefix for nouns, it sounds as if it has a short, soft *oo* in front of it, like the *oo* in *book*. If followed by *b* or *v*, the *oo* sound does not occur, and the *m* is not a separate syllable, except in words that contain only one vowel, e.g., *mti*
r	Different from the English, there is a bit of a trill on tip of the tongue
s	*s*it, never a *z* sound
bw	pronounced as a combination of the two sounds, but not separated (*bwana* is bwa-na, not bu-wa-na)
ch	*ch*eek
dh	*th*ough
gh	lo*ch*
mw	pronounced as a combination of the two sounds, but not separated (*mwalimu* is mwah-lee-moo, not muh-wah-lee-moo)
ng'	pronounced as in si*ng*, not fi*ng*er. Slightly nasal
ny	pronounced as a combination of the two sounds, but not separated, similar to the Spanish *ñ* (*nyani* is nyah-nee, not nee-yah-nee)
th	*th*ink, not *th*ough

In Swahili, the accented syllable is the one before the last.

When two different vowels are next to each other, each retains its own pronunciation. When two similar vowels are next to each other, they are pronounced as one long vowel.

Syllables always end with a vowel.

Nouns are divided into nine classes, and prefixes and descriptive words will change in order to agree with the noun classification. Therefore, the following glossary will include more than one form of a word for the same meaning, depending on which word it is referring to in the story. Please consult Hinnebusch, pp. 95-100, for further clarification.

Swahili	Pronunciation	Meaning
akili	ah-KEE-lee	clever
asali ya nyuki	ah-SAH-lee yah NYOO-kee	honey of the bee
asante	ah-SAH-ntee	thank you
bahati	bah-HAH-tee	luck
boga	BOE-gah	pumpkin
bustani	boo-STAH-nee	garden
buyu	BOO-yoo	gourd
chai	CHAH-ee	tea
chui	CHEW-ee	leopard
fisi	FEE-see	hyena
furaha	foo-RAH-hah	happy
hadithi	hah-DEE-thee	story
hapana kitu	hab-PAH-nah KEE-too	nothing
hapana mzuri	hah-PAH-nah m-ZOO-ree	not good
hodi	HOE-dee	May I come in?
hujambo	hoo-JAH-mbee	Are you well?
huruma	hoo-ROO-mah	kind
imekwisha	ee-may-KWEE-shah	finished
jaa	JAH-ah	full
kaa	KAH-ah	crab
kanga	KAH-ngah	cloth worn by women
karamu	kah-RAH-moo	feast
karibu	kah-REE-boo	You are welcome.
kidiri	kee-DEE-ree	ground squirrel
kidogo	kee-DOE-goe	small
kinyonga	kih-NYONG-gah	chameleon
kokwa	KOE-kwah	nut
kondoo na mbuzi	KOH-ndoe nah m-BOO-zee	sheep and goats
kubwa	KOO-bwah	large
kufa	KOO-fah	dead
kuro	KOO-roe	waterbuck
kuruka hewani	koo-ROO-kah hay-WAH-nee	fly
kwaheri	kwah-HEH-ree	goodbye
la	lah	no
maboga	mah-BOE-gah	pumpkins
mabuyu mawili ya mafuta	mah-BOO-yoo mah-WEE-lee yah mah-FOO-tah	two gourds of fat
macho	MAH-choe	eyes
machungwa	mah-CHOONG-gwa	orange
maembe	mah-EM-bay	mango
mafuta	mah-FOO-tah	fat

Swahili	Pronunciation	Meaning
maharagwe	mah-hah-RAH-gway	beans
maji	MAH-jee	water
mama	MAH-mah	mother
mamba	MAH-mbah	crocodile
mawi	MAH-wee	rock
mbaya	MBAH-yah	bad
mbili	MBEE-lee	two
mbogo	MBOE-goe	Cape buffalo
mbuni	MBOO-nee	ostrich
mbweha	MBWAY-hah	jackal
mdogo	m-DOE-goe	small
mfu	M-foo	dead
mgonjwa	m-GOE-njwah	sick
mimi	MEE-mee	I
miraa	mih-RAH-ah	a kind of tree
mjema	m-JAY-mah	good
mjusi	m-JOO-see	lizard
mkubwa	m-KOO-bwah	large
mmoja	m-MOE-jah	one
moja	MOE-jah	one
mtawala ya hewa	m-tah-WAH-lah yah HAY-wah	lord of the air
muhanga	moo-HANG-gah	aardvark
mvua kubwa	MVOO-ah KOO-bwah	big rain
mwezi	m-WAY-zee	moon
mzee	M-zay	male elder
mzungu	m-ZOO-ngoo	European; tourist
mzuri	m-ZOO-ree	beautiful; good
na	nah	and
nafahamu	nah-fah-HAH-moo	I understand.
ndiyo	n-DEE-yoe	yes
ngiri	n-GEE-ree	warthog
ngoma	n-GOE-mah	drum
ng'ombe wingi sana	n-GOM-bay WING-gee SAH-nah	very many cows
njingiri (Kikuyu, not Swahili)	n-jin-GEE-ree	ankle bells
nrefu	n-RAY-foo	long
ntupu	n-TOO-poo	empty
nyamaza	nyah-MAH-zah	silence
nyani	NYAH-nee	baboon
nyanya	NYAN-yah	tomato
nyumba	NYOOM-bah	house
nzuri	n-ZOO-ree	beautiful; good
paa	PAH-ah	gazelle
peke yake	PEH-kee YAH-kee	lonely
pole pole	POE-lay POE-lay	slowly
punda milia	POO-ndah MEE-lyah	zebra
rafiki	rah-FEE-kee	friend
raha na kimya	RAH-hah nah KIM-yah	peace and quiet
rangi ya mti	RAH-njee yah M-tee	color of the tree
rangi ya mwekundu	RAH-njee yah mway-KOON-doo	color of the earth
safari	sah-FAH-ree	journey
saidia	sah-e-DEE-ah	help
sana	SAH-nah	very
shimo	SHEE-moe	hole
shindano	shi-NDAH-noe	contest; race
shujaa	shoo-JAH-ah	hero

Swahili	Pronunciation	Meaning
si kitu	see KEE-too	It is nothing (you are welcome).
sikilizeni hadithi yangu	see-kee-lee-ZAY-nee haw-DEE-thee YAHNG-goo	Listen to my story.
simba	SIM-bah	lion
sungura	soong-GOO-rah	rabbit
swala pala	SWAH-lah PAH-lah	impala
tai	TAH-ee	vulture
tatu	TAH-too	three
tembo	TEH-mboe	elephant
toweka	toe-WAY-kah	invisible
tumbili	too-MBEE-lee	monkey
twiga	TWEE-gah	giraffe
ugali	oo-GAH-lee	porridge
ukosefu wa mvua	oo-koe-SAY-foo wah MVOO-ah	time of no rain
unakwenda wapi	oo-nah-KWEN-dah WAH-pee	Where are you going?
wangu	WANG-goo	my
watatu	wah-TAH-too	three
watoto	wah-TOE-toe	children
wawili	wah-WEE-lee	two
ya	yah	of
yangu	YANG-goo	my

Bibliography

Books

Adamson, Joy. *Born Free: A Lioness of Two Worlds*. New York: Harcourt Brace & World, 1960.

____. *Living Free*. New York: Harcourt Brace & World, 1961.

____. *Forever Free*. New York: Harcourt Brace & World, 1963.

____. *The Peoples of Kenya*. New York: Harcourt Brace & World, 1967.

Amin, Mohamed. *Cradle of Mankind*. Woodstock, NY: Overlook Press, 1981.

Amin, Mohamed, and John Eames, eds. *Kenya*. Englewood Cliffs, NJ: Prentice Hall, 1985.

Ashliman, D. L. *A Guide to Folktales in the English Language*. Westport, CT: Greenwood Press, 1987.

Bentsen, Cheryl. *Maasai Days*. New York: Doubleday, 1991.

Bierhorst, John, ed. *The Girl Who Married a Ghost and Other Tales from the North American Indian*. Collected by Edward S. Curtis. New York: Four Winds Press, 1978.

Bryan, Ashley. *Lion and the Ostrich Chicks and Other African Folk Tales*. New York: Macmillan, 1986.

Campbell, Joseph, and Bill Moyers. *The Power of Myth*. New York: Doubleday, 1988.

Carlson, Eric. *The Complete Book of Nature Crafts*. Emmaus, PA: Rodale Press, 1992.

den Boer, Afke, and Margot de Zeeuw. *Making and Playing Musical Instruments*. Translated by Anthony Burrett. Seattle: University of Washington Press, 1989

Eastman, Mary Huse. *Index to Fairy Tales, Myths, and Legends*. Boston: F. W. Faxon, 1937.

____. *Index to Fairy Tales, Myths, and Legends, Second Supplement*. Boston: F. W. Faxon, 1952.

Englebert, Victor. *Wind, Sand & Silence: Travels with Africa's Last Nomads*. San Francisco: Chronicle Books, 1992.

Fedders, Andrew. *Peoples and Cultures of Kenya*. Nairobi: Transafrica, 1979.

Fisher, Angela. *Africa Adorned*. London: Collins, 1984.

Fitzgerald, Mary Anne. *Nomad: One Woman's Journey into the Heart of Africa.* New York: Viking, 1993.

Gallman, Kuki. *I Dreamed of Africa.* New York: Viking Penguin, 1991.

Greaves, Nick. *When Hippo Was Hairy and Other Tales from Africa.* Hauppauge, NY: Barron, 1988.

Harris, Grace Gredys. *Casting Out Anger: Religion Among the Taita of Kenya.* London: Cambridge University Press, 1978.

Harris, Joel Chandler. *Complete Tales of Uncle Remus.* Edited by Richard Chase. Boston: Houghton Mifflin, 1955.

____. *Tales of Uncle Remus.* Retold by Julius Lester. New York: Dial Books, 1987.

____. *More Tales of Uncle Remus.* Retold by Julius Lester. New York: Dial Books, 1988.

____. *Further Tales of Uncle Remus: The Misadventures of Brer Rabbit, Brer Wolf, the Doodang & All the Other Creatures.* New York: Doubleday, 1990.

Haviland, Virginia. *North American Legends.* London/Boston: William Collins, 1979.

Hinnebusch, Thomas J. *Swahili: A Foundation for Speaking, Reading, and Writing.* New York: University Press of America, 1979.

Horrobin, David. *A Guide to Kenya and Northern Tanzania.* New York: Charles Scribner's Sons, 1971.

Huxley, Elspeth. *The Flame Trees of Thika.* New York: Viking Penguin, 1982.

____. *The Mottled Lizard.* New York: Viking Penguin, 1982.

____. *Out in the Midday Sun: My Kenya.* New York: Viking Penguin, 1988.

____. *Nine Faces of Kenya.* New York: Viking Penguin, 1991.

Ireland, Norma Olin. *Index to Fairy Tales, 1949-1972.* Westwood, MA: F. W. Faxon, 1973.

____. *Index to Fairy Tales, 1973-1977.* Metuchen, NJ: Scarecrow Press, 1985.

Ireland, Norma Olin, and Joseph W. Sprug. *Index to Fairy Tales, 1978-1986.* Metuchen, NJ: Scarecrow Press, 1989.

Iwago, Mitsuaki. *Serengeti.* San Francisco: Chronicle Books, 1986.

Kamante. *Longing for Darkness: Kamante's Tales from Out of Africa.* New York: Harcourt Brace Jovanovich, 1975.

Kavyu, P. N. *Traditional Musical Instruments of Kenya.* Nairobi: Kenya Literature Bureau, 1980.

Kenyatta, Jomo. *Facing Mount Kenya: The Tribal Life of the Gikuyu.* London: Secker and Warburg, 1938.

Kola, Pamela. *The Cunning Tortoise.* Nairobi: East African Publishing House, 1980.

Kyendo, Kalondu. *Cock and Lion.* Nairobi: East African Publishing House, 1969.

Maberly, C. T. Astley. *Animals of East Africa.* Forestburgh, NY: Hodder & Stroughton, 1984.

MacDonald, Margaret Read. *The Storyteller's Sourcebook.* New York: Neal-Schuman, 1982.

Maren, Michael. *The Land and People of Kenya.* New York: J. B. Lippincott, 1989.

Markham, Beryl. *West with the Night.* Berkeley, CA: North Point Press, 1983.

Martin, James. *Chameleons: Dragons in the Trees.* New York: Crown, 1991.

Matthiessen, Peter. *The Tree Where Man Was Born.* New York: E. P. Dutton, 1972.

McDermott, Beverly Brodsky. *Sedna.* New York: Viking Press, 1975.

McLean, Margaret. *Make Your Own Musical Instruments.* New York: Macmillan, 1982.

Muriuki, Godfrey. *Kenya's People: People Round Mount Kenya: Kikuyu.* London: Evans Brothers, 1985.

Mwangi, Rose. *Kikuyu Folktales: Their Nature and Value.* Nairobi: Kenya Literature Bureau, 1983.

Njoroge, J. K. *The Proud Ostrich.* Nairobi: East African Publishing House, 1967.

____. *The Greedy Host.* Nairobi: East African Publishing House, 1969.

Nzioki, Sammy. *Kenya's People: Akamba.* London: Evans Brothers, 1982.

Odaga, A. Bole. *Thu Tinda: Stories from Kenya.* Nairobi: Uzima Press, 1980.

Ogot, Bethwell A. *A Historical Dictionary of Kenya.* Metuchen, NJ: Scarecrow Press, 1981.

Omanga, Clare. *The Girl Who Couldn't Keep a Secret.* Nairobi: East African Publishing House, 1969.

Osogo, John. *The Bride Who Wanted a Special Present.* Nairobi: East African Publishing House, 1966.

Pavitt, Nigel. *Samburu.* New York: Henry Holt, 1991.

Perott, D. V. *Concise Swahili and English Dictionary*. London: St. Paul's House, 1972.

Roberts, John S. *A Land Full of People: Life in Kenya Today*. New York: Frederick A. Praeger, 1966.

SanSouci, Robert D. *The Song of Sedna*. New York: Doubleday, 1981.

Scott, Jonathan P. *Know Kenya's Animals*. Nairobi: Kenya Stationers, 1984.

Senoga-Zake, George W. *Folk Music of Kenya*. Nairobi: Uzima Press, 1986.

Stein, Conrad. *Kenya*. Chicago: Children's Press, 1985.

Waciuma, Charity. *The Golden Feather*. Nairobi: East African Publishing House, 1966.

Walther, Tom. *Make Mine Music!* Boston: Little, Brown, 1981.

Winslow, Zachery. *Kenya*. New York: Chelsea House, 1987.

Wood, Marion. *Spirits, Heroes & Hunters from North American Indian Mythology*. New York: Schocken Books, 1981.

Pamphlets

Kipsigis. Nairobi: Consolata Fathers. Distributed by Text Book Centre, Box 47540, Nairobi, Kenya.

Turkana. Nairobi: Consolata Fathers. Distributed by Text Book Centre, Box 47540, Nairobi, Kenya.

Samburu. Nairobi: Consolata Fathers. Distributed by Text Book Centre, Box 47540, Nairobi, Kenya.

Finally, read anything you can find at your library under Dewey Decimal System 398.2096!

Index

Photograph entries followed by an asterisk (*) have a full-color reproduction in the Color Plates section.

Acacia tree, 136(photo)
Adamson, Joy, ix
Akamba, 43-45, 48(photo)
   adaptation to Europeans, 44
   ceremonies of rites of passage, 43
   childhood, 43
   circumcision, 43
   crafts, 44
   creation myth, 43
   dwellings, 44
   elders, 44
   marriage, 43
   modern, 44
   naming of, 43
   stages of adulthood, 44
Amboseli National Park, 157

Baboons, 34(photo), 65
Baskets
   Akamba, 45
   Kikuyu, 9
"The Boy Who Went to Heaven," 14-17
   Notes and Tips, 19-20
   Translation, 18-19
Bre'r Rabbit, 11, 77-79, 133

Camels, 29, 32
Campbell, Joseph, 112
Casting Out Anger: Religion Among the Taita, 74
Cattle
   Akamba, 44-45
   Kikuyu, 6
   Samburu, 111-12
   Turkana, 29
Cheetah, 47(photo)
Childhood
   Akamba, 43
   Kikuyu, 4
   Kipsigis, 58
   Taita, 73-74
Circumcision
   Akamba, 43

Kikuyu, 4-5, 7
Kipsigis, 58
Luhya, 99
Samburu, 112
Taita, 73
Clitoridectomy
   Kikuyu, 4-5
   Kipsigis, 58
   Samburu, 114, 120
   Taita, 73
Colobus monkeys, 155
Cottar's Camp, 46-48, 154
Crafts
   Akamba, 45
   Kikuyu, 8
   Luhya, 99
Creation myths
   Akamba, 43
   Kikuyu, 3
Crops, 9, 45, 57, 73, 99, 111

Death
   Samburu, 115
   Taita, 76
Dik dik, 116(photo)
Donkeys, 29
Dwellings
   Akamba, 44
   Kikuyu, 6
   Kipsigis, 57
   Samburu, 111, 120-21
   Taita, 73

Eland, 77
Elephants, 77, 80(photo), 116, 126(photo)*, 153

Facing Mt. Kenya: The Tribal Life of the Gikuyu, 3-4, 8

Giraffes, 116, 153, 154(photo)*
"The Girl Who Couldn't Keep a Secret," 107

Gitema, Peter Kagathi, ix, 10, 11(photo), 46, 60, 101(photo), 118, 120, 122-23, 147-49, 151-52, 155(photo), 157(photo)
Goats, 6, 29
"Good Luck, Bad Luck," 126-30
  Notes and Tips, 133
  Translation, 131-32
Great Rift Valley, 120-21, 121(photo), 122-23

Harris, Grace Gredys, 74
Hyena and the Moon," 134-37
  Tips, 138
  Translation, 138
Hyenas, 12, 29, 48, 103-107, 117, 125, 129-33, 134(photo)*, 134-39, 157

Illness, Kikuyu, 7
Impala, 23(photo)*
Initiation
  Kikuyu, 4-5
  Kipsigis, 58
  Samburu, 112
  Taita, 73
  Turkana, 29-30

Jie, 29

Kagathi. See Gitema, Peter Kagathi
Kagathi, Winrose Waithira, 157(photo)
Kakamega Forest, 100, 102
Kalenjin, 57
Kapendo, 32
Karamojong, 29
Kebiro, Mogo wa, 8
Kenyatta, Jomo, 3, 8-9, 123
Kericho, 57, 60, 100
Kikuyu, 3-8, 11(photo)*, 12(photo)*, 13(photo)
  baskets, 9
  British, conflict with, 8
  cattle, 6
  childhood, 4
  circumcision (irua), 4-5, 7
  clitoridectomy, 4-5
  councils, 6-7
  creation myth, 3
  crops, 9
  dwellings, 6
  family structure, 3-4

  illness, 7
  initiation, 4-5
  justice, 7
  land ownership, 3-4, 8
  marriage, 5-6
  medicine man, 7
  modern, 9
  Mt. Kenya, 155
  music, 7
  polygamy, 6
  pottery, 8
  religion, 7
  sacrifice, 7-8
  seer, 8
  songs, 7
  storytelling, 7
  witchcraft, 8
Kinyangi, 32
Kipsigis, 57-58, 60(photo), 61(photo)*
  beer, importance of, 57-58
  childhood, 58
  circumcision, 58
  clitoridectomy, 58
  dwellings, 57
  four, significance of, 57
  initiation, 58
  modern, 57
  origin, 57
  ornamentation, 58
  religion, 58
  society, 57
  witch doctors, 58

Lake Nakura, 152(photo)
Lake Turkana, 29
Lake Victoria, 61, 62(photo)
Leopards, 46, 117, 118(photo)*
Lions, 22(photo), 33(photo), 34(photo)*, 46, 86(photo)*, 143, 149, 153
Luhya, 99, 101(photo), 102(photo)
  circumcision, 99
  crafts, 99
  migration into Kenya, 99
  modern, 99
  rainmakers, 99
  social structure, 99
  witch doctors, 99

Maasai, 111, 149, 150(photo), 154
Maasai Mara National Reserve, 46-48, 47(photo)*, 147, 149

Maps
    The Peoples of Kenya, endsheets
    Travels Through Kenya, xiv
Mara Serena Lodge, 149
Maralal, 119-21, 122-25
Markets, 100(photo), 147, 151
Marriage
    Akamba, 43
    Kikuyu, 5-6
    Samburu, 114
    Taita, 74
    Turkana, 30
Mau Mau, 8
Medicine man, Kikuyu, 7
Mombasa, 77, 153
Monkeys
    Colobus, 155
    Vervet, 89(photo)
"Monkey's Feast," 63-66
    Notes and Tips, 68
    Translation, 67
Mount Kenya, 4, 10(photo), 155(photo),
    156(photo)*
    Kikuyu creation myth, 3
    Ngai, 7
Mount Kiliminjaro, 153(photo)
Music, Kikuyu, 7

Nairobi National Park, 143
Naro Moru River Lodge, 10-13, 150, 156
Ngai, 7
"Not So," 33-37
    Notes and Tips, 40
    Translation, 38(Turkana),
           39(Samburu)

Old Stanley Hotel, 149
Omanga, Clare, 107
Omotic, 57
Ornamentation
    Kipsigis, 58
    Samburu, 113
    Turkana, 29
Ostrich, 81(photo)

Pavitt, Nigel, 111-12
"Peace and Quiet," 49-52
    Tips, 54
    Translation, 53
Photographs, taking of, 32, 123
Pokot, 29, 32
Polygamy, Kikuyu, 6

Pottery, Kikuyu, 8
The Power of Myth, 112

Rabbit, 21(photo)
"Rabbit and Lion," 21-24
    Tips, 26
    Translation, 25
"Rabbit and the Well," 32
"Rabbit's Drum," 80-82
    Notes and Tips, 84
    Translation, 83
Raymond, Susan Grant, x, 122, 125, 144,
    148, 152, 155, 156(photo)
Religion
    Kikuyu, 7
    Kipsigis, 58
    Samburu, 114
    Taita, 74-76
    Turkana, 30
Rhinoceros
    Black, 143
    White, 153
"Ripe Fruit," 103-104
    Notes and Tips, 107
    Translation, 105(Luhya), 106(Kikuyu)

Sacrifices
    Kikuyu, 6, 7, 8
    Samburu, 114
    Taita, 75
    Turkana, 30
Samburu, 111-15, 119(photo)*,
    121(photo), 124(photo), 125(photo)
    age sets, 112
    cattle ownership, 111-12, 113
    circumcision, 112
    death, 115
    dwellings, 111, 120-21
    elders, 114
    females, 114, 120
    food, 111
    initiates, 112-13
    initiation, 112
    marriage, 114
    origin, 111
    ornamentation, 113
    religion, 114
    superstitions, 115
    warriorhood, 113-14, 116,
          117(photo)*
Samburu, 111
Samburu Game Lodge, 116-19

Samburu River Game Lodge, 151
Sarova Lion Hill, 150
Sheep, 6, 29, 114
Southern Nilotic Group, 57
Stories, collecting, ix-x, 10-11, 12,
    31-32, 31(photo)*, 48, 60-61, 77,
    101, 117, 118, 119(photo), 123-25
Storytelling
    Akamba, 43
    Kikuyu, 7
Sunset Hotel, 151

Taita, 73-76, 78(photo)
    childhood, 73
    circumcision, 73
    clitoridectomy, 73
    death, 76
    dwellings, 73
    Executioners' Society, 76
    initiation, 73
    irrigation system, 73
    marriage, 74
    modern, 73
    origin, 73
    religion, 74-76
      anger, 74-75
      Figi, 75
      holy shrines, 75
      Kutasa, 74-76
      Mlungu, 75, 76
      rainmaking, 75
      rituals, 75

sere, 74
sorcery, 76
Taita National Park, 149
Tea, 60(photo)
Tea Hotel, 152
Tsavo National Park, 77
Turkana, 29-30, 31(photo)*
    athapan, 29-30
    crafts, 30
    diet, 29
    initiation, 29
    livestock, 29
    marriage, 30
    origin, 29
    ornamentation, 29
    religion, 30
Vervet monkeys, 89(photo)
Vulture, 49(photo)

Wanjala, Chris, 101
Warthogs, 88(photo)
"Water, Water Will Be Mine," 86-94
    Tips, 96
    Translation, 95
Waterbucks, 87(photo)
Wildebeest, 46-47, 46(photo)
Witchcraft
    Kikuyu, 8
    Kipsigis, 58
    Luhya, 99
    Samburu, 115
Wuaso Ng'iro River, 52(photo)

About the Author

Following the tradition of her grandfather, aunt, and mother, Heather is a third-generation storyteller who believes that stories are for all ages. Raised as an "army brat," she learned to enjoy traveling and experiencing different cultures and lifestyles. She planned to be an actress and received a degree in theater from the University of Missouri, Columbia. However, she soon realized that a love for stories was in her soul, so she acquired a master's degree in library science from the University of Denver and now is Head of Youth Services at the Edwin A. Bemis Public Library in Littleton, Colorado. Her storytelling performances have taken her across the United States, as well as to Africa and New Zealand. She lives in Evergreen, Colorado, with her cat, Oreo, visiting elk, deer, fox, raccoons, and hummingbirds, and enjoys the company of storytellers traveling through the area who will share their stories in exchange for a breathtaking view of the Rocky Mountains.